If These Ears Could Sing!

If These Ears Could Sing!

Michael James Gannon

DMF Publishing, LLC

"Imagination Is Everything"
It is the preview of life's coming attractions
— Albert Einstein

www.DMFPublishing.com
www.IfTheseEarsCouldSing.com
www.OfficialLawOfAttraction.com

If These Ears Could Sing!
By Michael James Gannon

Copyright 2011 by Michael James Gannon

This book is not intended as a substitute for psychological counseling or medical advice. The author and publisher disclaim any responsibility or liability resulting from actions advocated or discussed in this book. Those desiring or needing medical advice and/or counseling are encouraged to seek the services of competent professionals in those areas of expertise.

Published by:

"Imagination Is Everything"
It is the preview of life's coming attractions
– Albert Einstein

DMF Publishing, LLC
Reston, VA 20191

http://www.DMFPublishing.com

Printed in the United States of America

First Edition

ISBN: 978-0-9829235-0-4
Library of Congress Control Number: 2010935027

Cover design by Karen Saunders of MacGraphics Services:
http://www.MacGraphics.net
Interior page layout by Kerrie Lian, under contract with MacGraphics Services
Edited by Melanie Mulhall, http://www.DragonheartWritingandEditing.com
Author Photo by: Christopher Briscoe, http://www.ChrisBriscoe.com

There are significant moments when we realize that the people who walk beside us sometimes raise us higher than we could ever dream. We draw into our experience certain events, circumstances, and people who change the very fabric of our lives. I dedicate my book to Jeri Costa, a very rare person who has profoundly shaped and influenced the direction of my life.

Had I not attracted a spiritual crisis in my thirties, I would not have known or understood the dark night of the soul. If I had not prayed and listened to the inner promptings that led me to a spiritual event, I would not have crossed Jeri's path for the second time in my life. If I had not embraced the spiritual challenge that she courageously and masterfully guided me to explore, I would not have learned to transcend the defiance of my ego's grip. If she had not remained committed to a higher purpose, this book would not have been a reality. Her heart of gold, lively personality, and glorious sense of humor enriched the spiritual wisdom that led me down this path. It is here, in the telling of my story, that you will understand her cocreation and contribution in my life.

Jeri, clearly you are a godsend. I truly honor your divine magnificence.

Michael James Gannon

TABLE OF CONTENTS

AN IMPORTANT MESSAGE
TO THE READER

We are called to do great things with our life by the choices we make. Our thoughts and feelings are like inner missiles that propel us in the exact direction we have put out. However, we are not preconditioned to believe that destiny is a self-creation. We buy into the collective belief that what happens to us is the result of hard work, our gene pool, our upbringing, our life circumstances, and endless other explanations about what determines our life outcomes.

The law of attraction operates as a universal principle, despite our individual or collective certainty. So without knowing how negative thoughts and beliefs attract the opposite of what we want, we remain stuck. I invite you to redesign your blueprint. How would it change? Would you be doing something else, maybe something you loved? Would your relationships be more fulfilling? What if you could attract more wealth by changing your thoughts?

If These Ears Could Sing is not exclusively the "memoirs" of a deaf man. I tell the story of my life, with its myriad of ups and downs, struggles and triumphs, as an example of how we will always attract what we think and feel. I reveal how the universal "law of attraction" handed me back exactly what I was thinking and feeling about myself, regardless of my profound loss of hearing from birth. It is not a book of dos and don'ts or "how to," and there are no rules. It is a living testament to the consequences of both positive and negative thought and feeling.

In understanding this process, I have changed who I am and made possible the impossible. I hope that you will allow yourself to clear the slate, put aside your conventional beliefs, and decide for yourself. My promise in return is the knowing that whenever you are ready, your world will change because of who you are willing to become with this shift in thinking.

We are each the creator of our own life, with full access to an open doorway. This is where dreams are born. Leave the cocoon of imagination . . . *and defy the impossible!*

ACKNOWLEDGEMENTS

There are so many of you who have played unique roles in supporting me in writing this book. To all my family, friends, clients, and those who have offered me words of encouragement and inspiration, I am deeply grateful to each of you. I hope that you will share with me the thrill of seeing my book in print. *If These Ears Can Sing* has been a labor of love, learning, and growth. Without all of you, it would have had no meaning. I thank you from the bottom of my heart.

Jeri Costa, your contribution warrants its own page and I dedicate this book to you.

Sandy Morris, your heart energy was an indispensable contribution. Thank you so much.

Teri E Belf (http://www.belfcoach.com), your highly successful coaching certification program, Success Unlimited Networks, has given my career and life its greatest purpose. Thank you for initiating and galvanizing this book project.

Thank you Christopher Briscoe, (http://www.chrisbriscoe.com), for your excellent photography and shooting the best headshot for the cover.

Karen Saunders, owner of MacGraphics Services (http://www.macgraphics.net), finding you was the law of attraction at its very best. Your creative design rendition for my book cover was everything I hoped. And your supportive team of professionals in the publishing industry has been invaluable to me. You have a fan for life.

Melanie Mulhall of Dragonheart (http://www.Dragonheart-WritingandEditing.com), thank you for your incredible insight and talent for saying exactly what I thought I said. Melanie, to use your words, you made my words "sing and dance."

Thank you Linda Cook and Elizabeth Adams for your charitable time editing and advising me with my rough drafts with such spiritual wisdom and feedback.

Thank you Laurie Nelson and Brad Johnson of NM Productions (http://www.voiceanddrum.com). Laurie, I thank you so much for your talent as a singing coach and having the faith to see our voice lessons through. Brad, your rhythmic and creative grooves continue to inspire me to keep on drumming.

Claire Dwoskin, simply, you changed the course of my life. Thank you so much.

Advance Bionics, my sincere thanks for the amazing technology that has brought me the joy of sound.

Most importantly, words cannot express my profound gratitude for all I have experienced. I thank the Supreme Being, who blessed me with the creative power to give my dreams life.

A PRELUDE TO SOUND

chapter 1

Lost in a world of silence,

In a vacuum of noiseless sound,

I heard not even the faintest stirring of life.

If knowing were important to a newborn child,

I did not know my cries were shrill.

I did not know they were cries at all.

As shadows danced in a moonlit room,

My mother sang a sweet and soft lullaby.

I did not hear the love in her voice,

Nor the hushing whispers to ease away my baby tears.

I only felt the softness of her touch.

Trapped in walls of stillness,

Soundless only to me,

I was baby Michael James Gannon,

Ready to make miracles with my glad blue eyes.

Every baby born is an astounding expression, a vast orchestration and creation of love. But on October 9, 1959, the obstetrician called my birth "unremarkable," a clinical term used by the medical community to describe a normal birth and delivery. What a contradictory label to put on the miracle of life.

This medical notation of my birth would have gone unnoticed had it not been for the later developmental delays that indicated something might be wrong. I was baby number two, the second son of Bill and Peggy Gannon. My older brother, Brian, who was born one year and two weeks before me, sat up, crawled, walked, talked, and produced teeth as scheduled. Most of my mother's first time baby jitters belonged to the year that had already passed by the time I was born.

There would be three more births after me, and Brian would be the first and the last to be born without a disability.

Each month, with guarded anticipation, my mother brought me to the pediatrician for my well-baby checkup. I appeared to be a healthy physical specimen, but there was a tacit, lingering suspicion that I was lagging behind developmentally. Both of my parents recognized that Brian had been very different, and they resisted the obvious comparisons that left me behind.

"He will catch up," the doctor declared, politely reassuring my mother that I was fine and that every child had its own unique timetable.

My mother was not so easily convinced and my father was content to remain in denial until told otherwise. Of greatest concern were the distinct guttural noises that did not translate to excited baby coos on the verge of communicating sound. Neither parent mentioned how I arched my back like a serpent trying to spit his venom and then looked around frantically trying to connect. Neither parent mentioned that I was oddly distant and vaguely unresponsive to my surroundings. Both loved me, cared for me, held me, and prayed that things would change. They did not.

The enlightened sixth sense that tells a mother something is not quite as it should be continued to pull at the place where her maternal insight grew. Already she was pregnant with the third child and felt a greater urgency to know that everything was fine. Had she done anything wrong? Was there a genetic problem waiting to repeat itself before it was even recognized? Could it have been the diet pills they gave her to keep her weight down during her pregnancy with me?

Doug was born a year and a half after me, as if there were a yearly mating call to add another male Gannon to the brood. He was not an easy baby either and never seemed content. Even his sleep was fitful and his eyes fixated when he screamed hours on end. My mother was haunted by my seeming detachment from the outside world and now this new baby—who had also been deemed a healthy baby boy—demanded hours of soothing. With three children under the age of four, this was precious time she could not spare.

One thing she could count on from me was a smile that opened her heart and connected me to her when she held me close in her arms. In those moments she knew that everything would be fine, and it was the only certainty that mattered. It radiated like a beacon of light that would lead her to the truth . . . and it did.

By the age of two and a half, I did not talk or even enunciate a sound resembling speech. It is interesting that the word infant means "nonspeaking." It is believed that a profoundly deaf baby will connect to what is called "a phantom noise" rather than the aloneness and silence of nothingness. Most hearing babies are exposed to thousands of different noises on a daily basis, and no one knew or suspected that I did not hear them. My world was as quiet as a soundproof music studio. The lights were on, but the music was off.

One morning, just after breakfast, I sat in my high chair continuing to stuff dry cheerios into my mouth. My mother was tidying up the kitchen, while Brian noisily ran his cars over the table, onto the chairs, up the refrigerator, into the sink, and through the mess I had made on the floor. I was delighted to have my older sibling's attention and hurled my half-chugged baby bottle right at him. He shrieked as it caught him dead center in the back of his head and shattered on the floor. In her rush to attend to him, my mother knocked the cast-iron frying pan full of cold, congealed bacon grease to the floor. The unexpected clatter, enormous mess, and bump to his head evoked full throttle hysteria from Brian. I did not react at all to any of the chaotic sounds. I did not move in any startling fashion. I just continued to enjoy the remainder of my breakfast as if nothing could disturb me. In that moment of earsplitting pandemonium, my mother came to understand the truth.

A nurse friend of the family recommended an ear, nose, and throat specialist at Henry Ford Hospital in Detroit, Michigan. I was diagnosed profoundly deaf in both ears, which meant I heard nothing. She had spent restless nights awakened by the dread of the unknown. She had feared that I might be deaf and prayed for it not to be so. But it *was* so.

"Mike will be just fine," she had often said. But now she believed without hesitation that it was true. My dad was silently supportive even though unconditional acceptance did not come easily. He presented courage in the face of this challenge. He would need it.

I went through several months of being tested with earphones and hearing aids. Before my third birthday, I was provided with a box that amplified sound, to be worn around my chest. There was nothing available then that could be worn on my ears. The box was my only option.

Both of my parents remained dedicated in their efforts to help me speak, insisting that I communicate with words rather than point. Before I learned to talk, I would stand in front of the refrigerator, point, and utter some form of garble with great enthusiasm. It was a no-brainer: I wanted milk. This was the first declared battle of my own will over my mother's. She eventually decided that I needed to say the word before another drop touched my lips. It did not go well. When determined pointing no longer worked for me, I resorted to dramatic measures and hurled my body against the refrigerator. She would stoop down and gently speak into my hearing box, "Milk please." To her the word "please" was just as important as the word "milk."

I refused to budge, and so did she. There would be no compromise in this battle of wills. On the morning of the third day in the milk standoff, she came downstairs to begin making breakfast and have a peaceful cup of coffee. Daybreak had hardly peeked through the tilted shutters, leaving the room dimly lit. She glanced at the refrigerator. There I was, curled up on the floor in my feet pajamas with my blanket next to me, sound asleep. In my hand I clutched my plastic Pooh Bear cup, waiting for milk. This time, I had arrived first to the battleground. She had reached her breaking point. What kind of monster had she become? How could she refuse me even one more time? She reached down to pick me up and hold me in her arms. Tears streamed down her cheeks.

I looked up at her, my sleepy blue eyes not quite awake, and voiced the sweetest words she had ever heard. "Milk please." Soft but clear, I spoke for the first time.

It is said that a mother never forgets her baby's first words. Peggy Gannon inscribed these words on her soul, replayed them in her heart, and shouted them for the world to hear.

My parents enrolled me in a preschool for hearing-impaired children, even though they were determined that I learn to function as a hearing person. This program was innovative for its time and emphasized teaching deaf children to speak rather than use sign language. I was taught the sound of a letter, one at a time, and then learned to speak the entire alphabet. I didn't always articulate well, and many times refused to adapt to language as my way of communicating. There was a part of me that wanted to stay where I was safe, in a void with no sound. My mother was determined not to let that happen and persisted in making sure I pronounced words correctly. Unfortunately, for us both, I did not take correction well.

Whatever I lacked in my verbal skills, I made up for in play. I loved to be outdoors. I was well coordinated and very typically boy. I especially loved a romping game of toss using my hearing aid box as the ball. It was a nuisance tied around my neck, so if I threw it and kept it in motion, I would not forget it or leave it on the ground to be trampled. One day I got caught in action, and my mother stormed into the backyard like a heat-seeking missile and grabbed it out of my hand before I could throw it again. I did not need to hear her to know I was in trouble. On most occasions she bent down and gently spoke into the microphone located at my chest. Not this time. Without hearing a single word, I learned that a voice could be harsh and scary and that the box was not a toy to be randomly thrown in the air. How strange it felt to be reprimanded in silence while fighting back angry tears of frustration. Could it be that I was already forming a protective wall around my heart—the same location where my hearing device had gifted me with sound?

On a windy autumn afternoon, my father accompanied me to another hearing specialist. I was almost five years old and able to graduate from my chest-worn hearing aid box to behind-the-ear hearing aids.

"Where is Mommy?" I asked as Dad lifted me up on the cold metal examining table.

"Mike, you know she is at home with your little brother."

I did not hear him.

"I want her," I chanted over and over. Just as when I'd had a bad dream or my tummy ached, I wanted my mom. I hated people fooling with my ears, sticking things into them, looking with flashlights. Why couldn't they leave me alone? Why did I have to have ears anyway? The doctor had cold hands and long hairs growing out of his nose and I did not want him to touch me. Despite my growing belligerence, everyone around me was grinning like characters on my Saturday morning cartoons.

"Mike," the doctor said, "now we are going to turn on your new hearing aids." By his enthusiasm you would have thought he was about to tell me I never had to eat vegetables again. "Here we go!" he said as he turned it on.

And with that, I jumped straight off the table. In his zeal, he had forgotten to adjust the volume. It was on full throttle. The first sound that came screeching into my ears was a piercing, high, pitch-like whistle. My head was swimming in a pool of disoriented energy and felt almost detached from my body. After what seemed like hours of endless adjustments, we left. I walked out of the building, exhausted and glad I was going home.

The parking lot was lined with leafless trees. Only an occasional branch held on to its color. I stopped for a moment, and then continued to walk. Again I paused, only this time I was startled by another unsettling noise. I looked to my father to help decipher this strange sound. He knelt down next to me, not quite sure what I was referring to. I pointed to the leaves blowing in the wind. They were swirling around my feet and crunching as I kicked them to the curb. He then held leaves up to my ears and recreated the crackling sound. He also explained that there was this thing called wind and that it sometimes made a funny noise we could not see.

I reached down and grabbed some leaves in my hands. I discovered I could make them speak to me. I chased them as they flew along the ground and adhered to a chain-link fence. I loved the different smells and the adventure of the outdoors. My dad and I played rambunctiously, throwing leaves at each other and laughing until we couldn't breathe. When it was time to go, he took my hand and we crossed the parking lot to our car. I loved him so much.

That afternoon, my father realized that my shirt had always protected the microphone of my body-worn hearing aid and that I had never before heard the wind. He was deeply touched and couldn't help but wonder what else I had missed during those first years of life. Something big happened that day. We had formed a very special bond of understanding where feelings transcended the words to describe them.

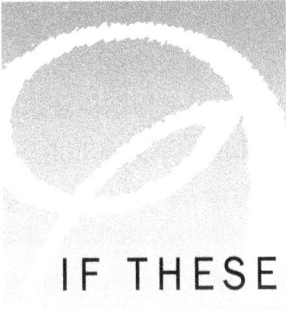

IF THESE EARS COULD SING

chapter 2

Over time, whenever I asked my parents what they experienced during those early years, I always sensed a guarded reply. Whenever I tried to elicit how they felt, rather than what they thought, it was as if feelings did not matter. Did they think that it might seem like a parent's betrayal to admit the pain and struggle, even within themselves? If so, I adopted their stance. I also learned to resist my own pain and stuff my feelings inside. I fought to maintain an image of invincibility, an image that fooled only me.

Today, when I think about the daunting silence that permeated my early childhood, I remember the many nights I lay in bed gazing at the shadows formed by moonlight. I relied on my eyes to ensure that I was in a safe place. In the late 1950s, the belief was that without the power of language there was very little reflective thought, because conceptualization of a thought form required the verbiage to describe it. My own childhood experience stood in opposition to this thinking and linguistic studies later proved it false. My world of thought—now, as it was then—has been the salvation of my life. Even without the language to describe the concept, thought kept me vibrantly connected to myself as a child. To this day, whenever I encounter a situation that calls for reflective thinking, I return to the lucid images and tranquility of my childhood bedroom, and a portal of understanding beyond my own wisdom unites me with my soul.

I was once asked, "Do you remember feeling lonely or scared as a small child when you heard no sound?" My first thought was that I'd had nothing to compare it with as a small child, because I had not known that sound existed. Yet I do remember the flurry of aliveness in this very silent place. This life force, this magnetic energy, was my earliest form of being "me" and I had no words to describe its vitality and power. I connected with others through sight and touch, never knowing the difference. There were many other things in those very early years that I can now understand from the perspective of a hearing world, but I had no understanding of them as they happened. However, I do believe that information was processed atypically in my brain as a result of my hearing and language deficit.

One of the first of these realizations came very unexpectedly. When I was home from college one summer, my parents decided to entertain us with some of the old home movies resurrected from our not so well preserved archives. I was stunned by the footage of my first birthday. It felt as if it was being played in slow motion and I was able to foretell each event before it unfolded. Somehow I remembered this day in uncanny but soundless detail. At first I wondered if this precise memory might have something to do with my having pushed my candled birthday cake off my high chair tray and onto the floor, which created a huge mess. But I have come to the conclusion that in the absence of hearing, my sensory awareness was coming predominately through my eyes, forming a lasting electrical imprint on my brain. My world was filtered through my vision and without the component of sound, my sensory awareness was likely retrieved from another place, a part of the brain where symbolic communication resides and where there is no historical perception of time. Even today, I rely on my visual acuity to remember precise detail because my auditory memory of an event seems more fleeting.

I also recall the first birthday party I was invited to and attended by myself. I was wearing my first behind-the-ear hearing aids. I could not wait to watch the birthday boy open the colossal pile of presents. I sat next to him and helped him rip into the packages. It was difficult for me to understand what people were saying with all the background noise, but I was having a wonderful time amidst all the excitement. His mother called us to the table to eat cake and ice cream. I wondered why there were candles on the cake. I knew matches and fire were forbidden territory for kids. At first, I was so enthralled with the fire that I did not notice there was a muffled sound all around me. Everyone's lips were moving at the same time, and they all appeared to be saying the same thing. I knew it was rude to talk when someone else was talking. I did not know they were all singing "Happy Birthday." I did not hear most music, so I had never sang a song. This event is my memory of the first time I actually knew and understood that I was different.

At the time, I thought, *If only these ears could sing, maybe I could be like everyone else.*

This daily battle for acceptance in the hearing world was an impossible fight for a little boy. How could I fit in, if even for an hour, and pretend to be just one of the guys? I longed to be a part of whatever sound did to include you on the playground, or that gave you passage to join in the chatter that made others smile. I would stand aside watching others engage in games, hoping to be included, yet afraid I would not hear the rules.

I remember trembling inside as I timidly asked, "Can I play?" I would often be ignored.

"Can I play with you?" I would say louder, thinking they might not have heard me.

They had heard me, but I was not like them. When I spoke it made them laugh, with hands cupped over their mouths, and turn from me like an animal shunned from the pack. They were only kids themselves. They neither felt nor knew that we were all the same . . . inside. I didn't know it either. I only knew it hurt to not fit in.

I did not understand the learned beliefs and prejudices that others had about deafness. This innocence sheltered me from some of the unwarranted cruelty. In those early years, I did not know that fat kids were left out and made fun of, or that wearing your pants jacked up meant you were a "geek," or that the color of your skin made any difference in how you were accepted. I never knew what whispering was, or that it could possibly be about me. I did not know that "rich" or "poor" were distinguishing factors related to where you lived or that you could not be anything you wanted when you grew up. My early conditioning never taught me about impossibility or that the childlike adventures that came to life in my imagination were not considered real.

I was happy to be alive in my inner silent world and was yet to understand that the hearing world had become a cruel intruder in my life and demanded my emancipation from deafness. My connection with my silent voice, and the wise observer that abided deep within, still knew that anything was possible. It was more audible than any voice I ever would hear as sound, but I had no way of knowing where it would take me.

We all have early childhood patterns that inhibit our sense of self-esteem. Yet, the more I lived from my own patterns and reacted painfully to what they brought to me, the more they seemed to show up in my life. I had no idea then that my own perception and judgments attracted more of the same. What I heard and understood, though negligible, became the cornerstone of my beliefs. The message came through loud and clear that I needed to please others to be accepted. I searched for gateways into the hearing world that would allow me to belong. The more I experienced frustration, the more frustration grew. There always seemed to be so much more I did not know. Even with my hearing aids, it was overwhelming to try to make any sense of what I heard. I was especially disheartened by a persistent ruffled, dense resonance that distorted conversation in the uncompromising drone of background noise. It left me bewildered in a maze of misconstrued words of seeming importance.

Yet there was relief from this dissonance when I turned off my hearing aids. It provided an escape into solitude and the return to a vivid imagination filled with joy. I kept this secret world to myself as it colored the daydreams of my life. It was a place of no judgment where I could be, do, and have anything I wished. I could create worlds of exploration in my mind's eye.

The inner world of my boyhood became a blessing in disguise, but it would be a much longer road before it became the source of my strength.

THE CHILD WHO DANCES IN MY EYES

chapter 3

Mom cradled her newborn son in her arms, exhausted but happy to finally have some alone time with him. Matthew Philip was the fourth baby boy born to our family.

She gazed outside through sun-washed windows barely aware that a world existed beyond this moment of solitude. It was unusually quiet. There were no babies crying. The racket of empty lunch trays being wheeled down the hall had subsided and the change of shifts gave a temporary reprise from intrusion. She treasured this privacy, knowing it would be short-lived. As much as she missed the rest of her brood, this was a welcomed break from the long days and nights ahead of her. She rocked the baby from side to side with a hypnotic rhythm that almost put her into a trance as Mattie began to stir and open his eyes.

Later she would tell us that in this moment, she felt an extraordinary love. Unlike the usual unfocused stare of an infant only one day old, these were eyes that knew her, eyes that held a presence she had never felt before.

Just hours before my parents were to bring Mattie home, the pediatrician arrived to give the final discharge orders. Mom listened intently to every word with her first baby, but she could have given the lecture herself by this time. Dad had just arrived with his camera in tow and the same going home outfit for the baby that we had all worn.

The pediatrician was not the same one they had spoken to the day Mattie was born. He introduced himself in a perfunctory greeting and sat down on the metal chair in the corner of the room, turning slightly so he could face them both. Mom was changing Mattie on the bed.

"I'm afraid I have some distressing news. Mr. and Mrs. Gannon, we believe your son has a congenital heart problem."

There was no warning to cushion the shock. He continued to speak, but his words did not sink in. With Doug and me, there had been inconclusive findings and long periods of waiting for answers, with only a mother's nagging intuition about what might be wrong. There was none of that this time. And this news was too devastating to be true. Surely not this time. Surely not this child.

"We suspect it is a cyanotic heart defect, a malformation that will require surgery later."

They had to be wrong. Hadn't they struggled enough? They had already suspected there were serious problems with Doug. I needed extra attention, special schooling, and a new audiologist. Where was the money coming from? How would they cope with the severity of this condition? Why had God done this to them? They pleaded with him for it to be a mistake, but the doctor's solemn pronouncement presented the bleak and sobering truth. It was not.

I needed no convincing that Mattie was a keeper. I was totally dazzled by this amazing network of fingers and toes moving in a fury of synchronicity, followed by stillness and what seemed like an eternity until he was awake again. I would gently pry open his eyes when no one was looking and then proclaim with great excitement, "Look Mom, he's awake!" His skin was a translucent white; pristine with the exception of the tiny blue veins that fought to keep him alive.

Mom would let me hold him if I sat down and I was transfixed with the responsibility of keeping him safe. Mattie became my devoted audience of one. From his first infectious giggle, I entertained him with superheroes, cops and robbers, and matchbox cars. It did not matter that my one-man production was often soundless. He loved the attention, as did I, when his smile suffused the entirety of his tiny face.

When Doug was born, I had been too young to comprehend that I was his big brother. He seemed to scream relentlessly and the possibility of a neurological-based finding loomed like thick smog, contaminating the horizon of his, and the family's, future. With Mattie's birth, that fog thickened a bit more.

Producing four children, one right after the other, was a decidedly Catholic accomplishment and no one questioned that our disabilities were God's will. Mom had been consistently pregnant since 1958. Her body was desperately thin, like a stray cat that had just delivered four litters of kittens. She endured many sleepless nights, and fear for her children stalked her many days. Did she ever resent the Church's dogmatic instruction that warned of the evils of birth control and denied her the possibility of choice? If so, she soldiered on without flinching.

Shortly after Mattie's birth, she became pregnant with her fifth child.

When Mattie was eight months old, the heart surgeons attempted a revolutionary procedure involving closed-heart surgery. By using one artery leading out of the heart into the lungs and then back into the heart again, the procedure would allow Mattie's blood to oxygenate twice before it was dispersed to the rest of his body. However, the doctors could not pass a catheter through because of extra tissue blocking the artery. They realized that his condition was atypical and discovered that his heart valves were not connected. He was diagnosed with a condition known as Tetralogy of Fallot, a three-part valve defect that limited sufficient blood flow to his heart and lungs. At only eight months, Mattie was too young to survive the type of heart reconstruction needed to correct the problem. The medical staff could only attempt to relieve the symptoms of labored breathing and poor circulation. Time became the enemy of life.

I never knew that Mattie was sick. I was far too young to understand about his heart. I only knew my own heart belonged to him.

Mattie's recovery was slow. I felt a very keen need for delicacy when I was with him. I could not play with him much, but it did not deter me. I became his self-appointed guardian and could not bear to see him cry or fuss. When he was almost two years old, we had one of the most devastating storms of the season. I kept telling him not to be frightened by the thunder. Of course it did not upset me because I barely heard it. The electricity was out everywhere, the flooded roads were closed, and the rain was relentless.

Amidst it all, Mother Nature had another event in progress. Mom was in labor and needed to get to the hospital as quickly as possible. Hours later, a flashlight's shining beam replaced the failed electricity and assisted in bringing forth the fifth Gannon child. The labor and delivery staff knew that she already had four male offspring at home. The very moment of delivery, the room shook—not from thunder, but from the collective scream, "It's a girl!" My mother had to have her own scrutinizing look to confirm that she had finally given birth to a girl. Tracy not only had the requisite anatomy, but she also had ringlets of dark, curly hair and electrifying blue eyes just like Mom. She was beautiful. Dad beamed.

You would think that by child number five, some of the excitement would have vanished. The stork had transported a baby to our house on an almost yearly basis. But he finally managed to bring us a girl this time. We couldn't wait to see her. Mom glowed as she walked through the front door with her new daughter in her arms. Tracy was dressed from head to toe in soft and flowing pink, declaring her female status among the Gannon male majority. We knew she would rule the kingdom.

My first act of subjugation to this diminutive monarch was a gift of great value to me. For years, I had been glued to my tattered silk beige blanket. I had absolutely no thought of giving it up. But when my mother tucked Tracy into her crib, I followed and tenderly covered her with my blanket, bestowing upon her my most prized possession. From that day on, it belonged to her. She kept it close, as I had, symbolically connecting us as brother and sister. We did not realize then that Tracy had also been born profoundly deaf. God had already linked us for life.

The enchantment of this darling little girl's arrival abruptly ended. When Tracy was only three weeks old, Mattie could wait no longer for a second heart surgery. As much as they had hoped for more time and prayed for his life, postponing the surgery was not an option. His breathing was labored and his color was a whitish blue. Mom felt an overwhelming sense of anxiety. How could she leave us, especially Tracy, a newborn baby? But then, how could she not be there for Mattie? How could she not hold the little hand that was always so cold from poor circulation? She knew how afraid he would be and knew that reassurances would never take away his pain. She recalled the inner knowing that brought her such joy the day after his birth. It was as if her heart beat in his body, her strength ran through his veins, and his soul—so new to this world—filled her with love and frightened her with the possibility of death.

I remember the morning Mattie left for the hospital. Grandma and Gramps had arrived the night before. We loved when they visited because it always meant the freshness of home-baked cookies, the warmth of a welcoming lap, and a lingering bedtime story. This time they were coming to take care of us while Mom and Dad were with Mattie. They did not tell us he was having surgery, only that he wasn't feeling well and they would take better care of him in the hospital.

"When is he coming home?" I asked.

"We don't know," Dad said.

"Why is he sick? Can't he stay at home?" I had become a relentless questioner. I was sure that we could take much better care of him at home.

"Kiss your little brother good-bye," my parents said, paying no attention to my insistence that he stay home.

I kissed him on his forehead and said, "I'm sorry you are sick, Mattie. I guess I will see you later."

My heart began to pound. Mom didn't know that I had seen the tears collecting in the wells of her eyes. They betrayed the smile on her face. I was already learning to perceive unexpressed sentiment in unspoken words. I watched out the living room window as they climbed into the old station wagon and disappeared into what seemed another lifetime. Brian wanted to play with Tracy's dolls. I got off the couch and threw up.

During the surgery, my parents waited anxiously, not knowing Mattie's condition, just that he was on a cold metal table with his heart exposed and desperately clinging to life. Dad, who had always been so strong, began to tremble. He would not even think of the possibility of losing his child. He could not take a breath, because any movement would shake the very foundation that held him together.

A doctor finally appeared with news.

"Mr. and Mrs. Gannon, your son is out of surgery and he is stable."

Mom and Dad both wept tears of elation. Mattie opened his eyes and hope was revived until a dreaded call from the hospital at 3:00 a.m. Matt was in acute cardiopulmonary arrest. Not wanting to wake Grandma and Grandpa, Mom drove alone to the hospital. By the time she reached him, he was breathing on a respirator and remained in critical condition. Having him in intensive care was frightening enough, but he was placed in isolation to reduce the risk of infection. Mom could not see him or hold him.

He remained there for thirty days, barely hanging on to life. Each day they did not know if we would ever see him again. Mom and Dad took turns at the hospital with him. They were torn between caring for their children at home and being with Mattie. They said little, not wanting to alarm us, but Mattie's crisis changed them. The rawness, sadness, and helplessness of it took its toll. I did not understand then how pain inevitably burrows into the unconscious mind and remains the dormant prey for unresolved anger.

I missed him terribly and I did not understand why no one would talk about when he was coming home. One day, almost six weeks later, Mattie came home and I could only stare in disbelief at the small shell encasing the fragile being that was my brother. He shivered uncontrollably as he waited for a clean pair of flannel pajamas. For the first time, I saw the gaping stitch lines crisscrossing his chest, wrapping around both sides of his ribs to the back of his spine.

"What happened to Mattie?" I screamed.

"Mike," Mom said, "Mattie had to have surgery to help him breathe better. It is okay now."

I knew better. It was not okay. It would never be okay again. I could see that he had almost been cut in two. How could that possibly be okay?

"Will he die, Mom?"

"No, Mike!" she replied with force. "No."

How did I know about dying? Hadn't my deafness shielded me from knowing about the cruelty of death and how it could take us away? I ran from the room to cry, to return to the silence that protected me from what I did not want to hear. I held my teddy bear tightly—the one with the button nose ripped off—and rocked until I lulled myself to sleep. Mom never came to comfort me. She had no energy left for my tears, not now, not this time.

Despite his lengthy recovery, Matt was well enough to participate in his first Halloween outing. Bozo the clown was his absolute idol. I watched his excitement grow as Mom found the perfect outfit, with a ruby red nose that squeaked. I masqueraded as Bugs Bunny, deciding that I would rather have his large ears. Maybe then I could hear. The skies were filled with flickering stars that seemed to light the way for trick-or-treaters in their relentless quest for candy. We lived in a row house neighborhood filled with baby boomers. There were kids galore—witches, ghouls, goblins . . . and one little Bozo the Clown, laughing and having the time of his life. It was so heartwarming to see him have fun after the pain of his surgery.

When it was time to call it quits, we sorted and traded our candy before Mom confiscated it to be doled out rather than eaten at once. I sat next to Matt while we unloaded our pumpkin bucket and dug into our collection with mouthwatering vengeance. Slobbering chocolate, you would have thought we had won the lottery. In many ways we had.

I had put to rest the horror of seeing Matt's disfigured body. I had forgotten the scars that had frightened me to tears and the futile longing for answers as to why he was sick. My memory at that time seemed wired to forget any trauma that I could not face. Still, Matt's brush with death had changed us all. Having experienced the threat of losing my brother, I was less trusting. But that night I was caught up in the moment. I forgot that he had ever been sick. We were brothers wearing the disguise of characters we loved. Nothing else mattered.

One day after school, for some unknown reason, it struck me that Matt always sat down while playing. He would only watch while the rest of us ran around. I decided to experiment. I took him by the hand and ran with him around the front yard, pulling him slightly behind me as fast as his little legs could travel. To my surprise, he did quite well. I had never seen him so animated. It was as if he had escaped from an invisible prison wall that held his body captive. I decided to go faster. He could hardly breathe but he did not care as he flew with me for the very first time. We both screamed with excitement, which my Mother immediately heard from an open kitchen window.

She tore out the front door and screamed, "Mike, you cannot do that to Mattie."

I was startled and frightened by the horrified look on her face. What had I done? She picked him up and ran into the house. I followed behind.

"Mom, we were just playing!"

"Mike, you cannot do that with Matt!" she replied tersely.

"Why?" I asked hesitantly.

"Well, his heart is not strong enough to run."

"But why?" I could feel my strong resistance against accepting this kind of limitation.

"Mike, you know Matt has a bad heart and he is not physically able to move much."

"But he ran, Mom. Didn't you Matt?" I said, looking to him for support. "He can do it! Mom, I saw him."

"No, Mike," she said with greater determination. "He cannot run and you must never ever do that again! Promise me now that you won't."

I knew she meant it and I was ashamed that maybe I had hurt his heart.

"Will he ever be able to run Mom? Will he?" I pleaded, feeling totally vulnerable.

"We can only hope at this point," she said.

It was the deep, reserved yet fragile look on my mother's face that made me feel how real this was and how small and vulnerable her voice sounded as it trailed off wistfully.

"Sorry, Mom, I just wanted to play and run with him, that's all."

She looked at me with a momentary smile of forgiveness that quickly changed to a stern expression that reinforced her words that it must never happen again.

I can remember feeling a sense of defenselessness, a guilty susceptibility that left me shaken. It felt deep and worrisome. I just stood there totally immersed in the moment, upset by the reality of limitation. I didn't want to believe that he couldn't do much of anything. I felt a sense of personal disloyalty accepting the likelihood that Matt had restrictions that would hold him back. I refused to accept that all things were not possible. And so I persisted, not giving up until I had a solution. I decided I was going to involve him in whatever physically strenuous activity I engaged in without actually having him participate. If he could not do it himself, I would do it for him. I would show him how it was done for now and get him ready for the day he could run and play.

It worked. I noticed how wide-eyed and energized Matt became after I engaged him in watching my antics. I would run as fast as I could and dive headfirst into a big pile of leaves or hang from a tree that was twice as high as the house. Matt sparked my imagination to push the limits of chance, and these daring feats riveted him. The more entertained and astounded he was, the more I wanted to amuse him. It was through me that Matt was able to live and experience a physicality that his condition had taken away. And it was through him that I learned never to give up, and never to say "No" without an alternative plan for "Yes!"

There were many days when my mother was fatigued from the endless running around, driving each of us to wherever we needed to go. Through it all, Mattie remained by her side. When my grandparents visited, Mom treasured the luxury of being able to take a nap. Mattie would lie down with her, even if he did not sleep.

One afternoon, after a particularly hectic day, she said to him, "Would you mind if I took a nap alone today?"

I will never forget the look on his face. He just gazed at her, motionless, as if a piece of him was about to be taken away. In a surrendering voice, he replied, "Are you sure, Mom?"

She kissed him on his forehead and walked up the stairs. After an hour and a half, she arose from a deep and restful sleep. There was Mattie, her little angel, sleeping three steps up from the bottom of the stairs. He had waited for her, knowing and trusting that she would never leave him. He would wait for her.

As Matt became older, his endurance became more and more encumbered. By the age of five, he was developing sleep sweats due to oxygen deprivation and had to undergo his third operation. Unlike the second surgery, the third went relatively smoothly. The postoperative recovery period was difficult, but not as critical as it had been only two short years before. Sadly, despite the surgery, he continued to deteriorate. He was not the same Mattie who watched me play, who giggled late at night, and who had, in many ways, become my ears. He had grown more quietly present, more withdrawn. As he approached his sixth birthday, his appetite began to dwindle and his wasted little body was clammy to the touch.

My parents knew time was running out and he would require more surgery. One night I heard them talking about how they wished they could buy him more time, with the hope that with each passing day, technology would advance enough to save him. I proudly offered my savings of $20. Surely I could buy that time. We could all save our money if that is what it took. Didn't they know that?

My mother was a determined woman and she looked all over the country for the best surgeon to take Matt to the next level of stability. As it turned out, a world-renowned heart surgeon from the University of Minnesota had relocated to New York and brought with him a dedicated following of skilled physicians. My parents met with him several times and decided it was time. This surgery promised to be more than a temporary measure. If all went well, it offered a lasting solution. Although precious time could not be bought, as I had hoped, science had made advancements in its ability to correct his deteriorating condition.

I again became relentless in my questioning. "Why does he have to go for more surgery? Why does he have a bad heart anyway? Why can't I see him and be with him in the hospital?" Not only did I probe my parents with questions, I also kept asking myself the same questions over and over again. *Why did he hurt so much?* I was drowning in a sea of questions. Each wave of questions had no answers, which spawned frustration and drove me further away from hope. I dreaded the day he would leave for the hospital, knowing that his chest would bear yet another telling scar that would further disfigure his torso. This time I was really frightened. I had to face my helplessness and I hated it!

When the day arrived and Mattie had to leave, he came up to me looking very sad. I could hardly look at him. I couldn't go through it again, not this time! I wanted to hide him somewhere where no one would find him, where they would not be able to take him away. He would be safe with me. He hung his head down; his hands limp by his side.

"Mike," he said, "I might not be coming back."

I was frozen and unable to speak. I darted up the stairway, not looking back. My parents came up behind me. They had not heard his words, and they were totally unaware of what had just transpired. I stared at them in utter contempt and refused to return the kisses they left upon my cheek.

Later, I heard the front door close below. I tore downstairs to watch them walk hand in hand down the driveway and towards the yellow cab that would take them away. I watched them get into the car, drive away, and disappear. I never once took my eyes off my little brother until they were completely out of sight. I began to tremble and cry from a place so deep that it did not feel it belonged to my body. I was not yet ten years old, but I somehow knew that my life was about to change profoundly.

It was too great a distance for my parents to commute daily from our home in Connecticut to the hospital in New York, so my Grandma and Grandpa stayed with us while my parents were gone. I knew they would call with periodic updates, but I did not expect to see them until Matt came home.

On September 27, six days after Matt left for the hospital, I went straight to the kitchen for something to eat after school, as usual. Grandma fixed me a sandwich, but she seemed very preoccupied and not herself. I loved talking to her and chatting about my day, but she insisted I find something to do. As I immersed myself in *The Andy Griffith Show*, I noticed a taxicab pull up in front of the house and I saw Dad and Mom get out with their luggage. I yelled out to Grandma that they were home. She insisted that I stay put while they collected their things and made their way into the house. As they walked towards the front door, I noticed that Matt was not with them.

"Grandma, where's Matt?"

"Just wait here honey. Your mom and dad will be here in a moment."

She sounded a bit taken aback, which triggered for me an odd, slow motion feeling of dread. Mom came in first and gave me a detached hug.

Dad followed close behind and said, "Hi, Mike," in a soft, reserved tone.

My mother immediately went up the stairs and disappeared.

Dad called out for Brian to come to the living room. He sat down in his favorite chair and pulled us close to him on opposite sides. I was leaning on his right leg and Dad had his left arm around Brian. Everything became very real, very quiet. Doug and Tracy were nowhere in sight.

"Dad, where's Matt?" I asked.

He choked on his words and his eyes welled up with tears. I started to shake. Brian remained motionless. Dad could not speak.

"Dad?" I repeated.

"Mike, your brother will not be coming home."

"What do you mean he's not coming home? Where is he going?"

"Mike, he passed . . . your brother passed away."

Tears started to stream down my father's face. Don't ask me how I knew what that meant but I did. I gasped! I quickly looked around the room, not knowing what I was looking for.

"You mean he's never coming back?"

Dad nodded ever so slightly in acknowledgement. I felt a sinking yet crushing rush in my chest. At first I could not utter another sound. I was paralyzed in disbelief. And then a volcanic rumble of emotion, a deep stirring from within my body, gathered momentum and resounded into a desperate cry.

"Noooooooooooooooo!" I screamed, releasing the unbearable, unthinkable pain.

I gasped for air.

"Mattieeeeeeeee! Daddddddddd, nooooooooooo!"

The sound was primordial, an anguished howl that I heard in my inner voice and expelled through my lungs. It was not containable. There would be no comfort or hug or holding that could release me from my despair. Death was pillaging my soul. I kept looking back and forth between Dad and Brian, and then around the room for Matt, oblivious and disengaged from any reality. Brian didn't shed a tear. He seemed unmoved, as if he had heard nothing of what was said. He stared vacantly, his eyes empty, disconnected from all emotion . . . disconnected from his heart.

I ran up to my room and closed the door behind me. I fell on my bed and cried until there was nothing left but the unrelenting ache in my heart. Grandma came in to be of comfort, but I knew there would be no reassuring because nothing would ever be the same again. I had told Mattie not to go and he knew when he left he wasn't coming home. Of course, he *had* gone home, but I didn't understand that then.

There was movement and activity around me, but nothing registered for a time. Sometime later, sitting on the window ledge of my parents' bedroom, I stared out the window towards the twilight sky and crumbled beneath it.

"God, pleassssse bring Mattie back to me! Mattie, please . . . please come back!" Not wanting to accept the impossible, I added, "I know you can!"

Out of the corner of my eye I saw my mother with tears streaming down her face. She couldn't handle the deep sobs of her helpless child on top of the profound pain of losing his brother. She could not look at me or hold me. She went to Mattie's room, where everything was still the same, where his little boy smell and favorite toys remained untouched and where her broken heart could summon strength for the days ahead.

I was told I was going to see Matt one last time. I had never seen a dead body. I didn't know what to expect. The drive to the funeral home meandered through unfamiliar streets, to a place where they were keeping Mattie, dead and away from us. I watched out the window, hoping that we would be told it was all a mistake, that he would be coming home and that we could turn around.

That did not happen. When we pulled into the parking lot, it was full of cars. Our relatives and friends had come to say their good-byes. As we entered the funeral home, the room was full of people. I could see the open casket in the back and knew it held my little brother. Relatives and friends were coming up to express their condolences. I was trying to hold back my tears, waiting for the moment I would see Matt one last time. Then the room became quiet. The wake was about to begin.

My mother led all of the kids towards the casket, beginning with Brian. I could barely hear the eerie sound of death music that was meant to comfort us and bring us peace. It did not. I could not bring back what I wanted most—my little brother. I wanted to scream, "Please stop, and make it go away." Brian looked at Matt, transfixed. After a few moments, he walked away. Still no tears. I thought to myself, *I wish I were that brave*, but I knew I wasn't.

Then came my turn. I felt like I was in a bubble of silence, feeling everybody's eyes of sorrow burrowing into my heart. As I walked up the aisle, the silhouette of his body slowly came into full view as I neared the casket. He was wearing his favorite red and black checkered shirt and he was much smaller than I had remembered him being only a week earlier. He did not move. I silently begged him to move.

Please move, Mattie. Come on, you can do it!

I looked very closely at his chest, hoping for the impossible, the slightest chance that he might take another breath and open his eyes. I wanted to touch him, but I was afraid I wasn't allowed to. I did not know the rules of being dead. And then fear crippled my own aliveness and I could not move or speak. My throat started to choke up. I realized this was it. I was never going to see him again. I couldn't hold it in anymore and I wept my last good-bye.

"I love you Mattie!"

There he was, etched forever upon my memory. I looked at him and knew that this would be the most devastating loss of my life. The brother I so deeply loved, the one friend that had meant the world to me, was now gone. God had come to take him to a place I could not go.

ℰℭℰℭℰℭℰℭℰℭ

As I write this, tears run down my cheeks. Yet, I've become aware that it is not the pain of loss that has grown with time, but the depth of my love for him. Matt was more than my little brother. He was a kindred soul that never dies.

There were lessons that his death imposed. It was not until I reached adulthood that I learned how my childhood wounds impacted my reactions to later external events. I have learned how suppressing my pain kept me from feeling my emotions and vulnerability. I learned that playing it safe is a short-term fix that only contributes to long-term emptiness and lack of fulfillment. Mattie's death unknowingly built a wall of protection around me so impermeable that it took years to tear it down, piece by piece. I realize that it was not the acceptance of his death that set me free; it was learning to surrender to my heart that allowed me to feel again. I know that he had been able to live his abbreviated life vicariously through me by what I had been able to show him in the physical world. When he pretended to climb the highest mountain of his dreams, I called him "Mighty Matt."

To Mighty Matt:

As I reach the summit of my own life, I know you will be waiting on the other side of the mountain. But for now you are and always have been . . . The Child Who Dances In My Eyes.

THREE STRIKES AND YOU'RE OUT
chapter 4

After Mattie died, I was relentless in my search for certainty about death. I demanded proof about this place called heaven, but even the questions seemed forbidden territory. How did everyone seem to know he was in a much better place with God and the angels? The only image of God I could resurrect was that of an old man with a flowing white beard surrounded by corpulent babies with feathered wings. I had seen this image painted on our church walls. How would they take care of Mattie? I knew he wouldn't like such a place. I thought about him being alone, buried in the cold ground. He had been terrified of the dark. How long would he have to stay in that box, with only a granite stone marking his life? Why wouldn't they check his grave and make sure he had really gone to heaven? How were they so sure? I could sense the uncertainty in my parents' voices and the remote look in their eyes. They would have taken him back in a second. They really did not know for sure any more than I did. They wanted me to believe he was in God's hands, but they had not been to heaven and back.

When I closed my eyes I could conjure up his smile, I could hear his silent laugher transmute all sound, and I could feel the love for him in my heart. If I wanted "aliveness" to reclaim him, it had to happen within me. I was desperate to stop my feelings of helplessness and vulnerability about death because they were drilling a hollow in the pit of my stomach. I was alone with my confusion and, to make matters worse, my fondest memories inflicted grief.

In the naked innocence of childhood, I discovered that my thoughts were real. They could move me beyond pain, they could take me to places that did not otherwise exist, and they would always bring me back to the safety within. It did not matter if no one else believed me. I believed me.

I needed a playing ground and game plan for Matt's life and baseball seemed the perfect venue. We played for hours in this heaven. Matt was strong and fast and I could hear the ball whiz by at ninety miles an hour. We had a great record on the mound. We won, we lost, and we played every position on the team. There are strict codes and rules in any game and that is how I rationalized his death. His first two surgeries had been strikeouts and when they wielded the knife for the third time, he struck out again and the game was lost. I replayed every scenario that might have saved him, but we knew the rules and there was always another game. I would be there to cheer his every home run. Together we were unstoppable. No one and no thing could ever say no to my daydreams. I created a heaven I could understand and relate to. Mattie could always come along for the ride or, as an angel with wings, he could simply fly away.

As much as this belief became my solace, there is always another side to the story. We were all changed by Mattie's premature death. As a family, nothing was ever the same and, oddly, we did not speak of it to each other. We all felt the unspoken angst of having lost the most precious member of our family. We never said the words "I matter less," but unconsciously, we all felt it. This painful feeling not only resided in our hearts, it also manifested as part of our collective experience. Mom's eyes would often be red from crying and her hugs, once warm and inviting, had become feeble and devoid of feeling. She withdrew to a private, empty place, unknown even by Dad. No one recognized the deadly depression that consumed her life. I watched my father bury himself deeper in his work, and the bright spark that had once shone in his eyes dimmed in the face of death.

Of course, our unwanted feelings attracted into our experience that which consumed us. We were unaware that feelings melded into our energy fields and reproduced themselves in the blueprints of our lives. Within my own inner self I could have changed how I felt, but I often turned a deaf ear to the voice that reminded me.

In fourth grade, I was placed in a music class for the first time. My hearing aids did not have the power or range to pick out the notes. I was told I would learn to appreciate the various instruments and the role of music. Like most boys my age, I zoned out and regarded it as a stupid class. When it came to singing, I never understood most of the words or heard the musical accompaniment.

Thankfully, I had neither heard nor figured out that we would be performing in a concert in front of the entire school. When that day arrived, I was totally taken by surprise and panicked. Was this a cruel joke? Did it even occur to them that a deaf kid couldn't sing? After years of speech therapy, being able to talk seemed like it should be enough. I had a flashback of the cartoon characters I could see on television. I could not understand because they had no lips for me to read. Now I would look just like one of them, moving my lips with my sound button off. I walked on stage in front of the entire student body, my heart pounding wildly before I realized I could fake it. I would randomly move my lips and hope that from a distance, no one would know the difference. It worked! At first, I was pleased with myself that I had seemingly pulled it off, but then it angered me. I waited until the next music class, and as soon as it began, I marched straight to the principal's office.

"Did you know I cannot hear?" I said.

"Why of course," she said, both of us knowing full well that I was the only deaf kid in the school.

"Then why am I in a music class with sounds I cannot hear?"

I was beginning to tremble inside. Like a silent mantra that would keep me brave, I kept telling myself, *I won't stop!* I remembered all the times I had learned by observation rather than by hearing, so I asked her to come back to the class with me because I had something to show her. As we walked into the classroom, the teacher was playing the piano.

I took a bold chance and said, "Do you know what note she is playing by the sound it makes?"

She listened for a few measures. "Well, not really," she responded honestly. I had never considered the possibility that she might say she did.

THREE STRIKES AND YOU'RE OUT

"Well then how am I supposed to know how it sounds when I can't even hear it?"

She looked back at the music teacher and rose from her seat, then told me to come with her back to her office. She invited me to sit down. *Here it goes*, I thought. *She is calling my mother to tell her how boldly I had spoken to her.*

She looked at me with the kindest eyes and said, "Mike, I am so sorry this happened to you and I am so proud of you that you were able to tell me. When you have music class from now on, you are to report to my office and use this time to study or read if you like. However, if ever there is a time when you want to go back to class, you can let me know."

There was no scolding and no "teacher knows best" lecture. I was emancipated. This experience taught me that when I spoke with conviction, I did not need the perfection of a perfectly formed sentence or the choice of the right word. A genuine heart could stand alone. She knew there was value in having me in that music class and that one day I would be ready. But she also knew that there was greater value in honoring how I felt.

My freedom to leave that class did not close a door, it opened one. I began to fantasize myself singing. I could hear myself hum as the melody filled my inner voice. I never told anyone that when I turned off my hearing aid, sometimes I heard the most beautiful music. I had a warm connection with these sounds and I secretly loved it! As I got older, the shower became my escape. So with the hot water steaming and pounding on my chest, I bellowed whatever sound resonated from my heart. It was always a perfectly orchestrated creation of beauty. After all, I was stone deaf and did not know the difference. One thing I knew for sure, it sounded nothing like the bellowing of a fourth grade choir. Beginnings are found in unsuspected places, under stones that eventually turn over and show the other side. Through singing, I started to believe that anything was possible and what started out as absurdity could be transformed.

When I was eleven, many of the kids in my class were on a Little League Baseball team named The Cobras, so I joined. I liked being on a team, but most of all, I liked being accepted as one of the guys and loved the camaraderie. I was the starting pitcher with well deserved bragging rights for my curveball. My fastball wasn't too bad either and I exhibited excellent hand-eye coordination. I was coming into my own and showing adeptness for athletics. After an incredible season, our team made it to the Westport Little League Championship finals. We were unwilling to lose.

It was the last game of the series. I felt brazen, yet at the same time, I felt apprehensive about making a fatal mistake. I threw a few wild balls at the plate and the walks were ratcheting up. The coach gave me one of those looks that needed no words. I knew this was the moment. I had to stay focused on pitching well. The noise on the opposing team was getting louder and more distracting. I could feel the energy swinging in their favor and yet I could viscerally feel my own gut screaming, *No way! We will win this!* It was as if I had a direct line of communication with that big baseball field I envisioned in the heavens. My inner voice spoke loud and clear. *Turn down your hearing aid and drown out the distraction of the opposing team. Yes! I will not hear you!* I screamed inside, grinning from ear to ear. Instantly cut off from sound, I could hear only me—that childlike, silent voice of deafness that could calm me from the inside out. I felt startlingly in charge, cut off from the distraction and jeers of onlookers. At the bottom of the sixth inning, the opposing team was at bat with two outs and two men on bases. We were up by one run and holding. I remained in the quiet zone.

"Strike one!"

There was visible apprehension on the opposing team.

"Strike two!"

I could feel the shift, the energy started to swing back in our favor.

"Ball one."

It did not deflate me.

"Foul ball!"

Aw, come on! Let's go! Put this baby over the plate!

I felt a strong surge of assurance going through me. I knew I had it licked. *Mattie, this one is for you!* I focused on the catcher's mitt and stole a momentary pause to make eye contact with the batter. I waited until he knew I was sending him an unequivocal message, and then I gave him a little one-sided grin. The moment he looked puzzled I threw the pitch.

"Strike three!"

And it was over! The whole team was delirious! We were the Little League champions of Westport, Connecticut. That experience taught me that when the going got tough, I could turn down the volume and switch out the negativity. I could draw from my inner silence and connect to an affirming energy that proclaimed, *You can do it!*

I knew what it meant to compensate and make the best of it. Three strikes and you're out belonged to the game of baseball. It was not a rule of life.

GAME CHANGERS

God, heaven, and the baseball field were about as far as I had come in my spiritual development until my preparation to make my First Communion in the Catholic Church. This catechism class had kids from all over in one huge classroom, as well as the enigma called nuns. Not only did they disrupt my Friday after-school playtime, but they were also a force to be reckoned with, allowing zero tolerance for nonsense.

I decided to remain as quiet and inconspicuous as possible. For once, no one seemed to recognize that I was in the class. I just blended into the rows of kids who nodded yes to the nun. I grasped enough to understand that we would all get dressed up, boys in blue and girls in white, and parade into church together. We would receive a white wafer, put into our mouth by the priest, and it would make us holy. Since I already knew kids who had done this, and they were not "holy," I assumed that it did not always work. However, I had no idea about the practice of going to confession. That part had just slipped through the cracks of my hearing deficiency and my inattention.

On the Friday afternoon before the big day, I just showed up as usual for the regular session and we filed into the church for what I assumed was another practice. However, this time, all the boys were ushered into a single-file line on one side of the church and the girls on the other. It was a good thing I was not first because these were confession lines. Each kid would disappear into a booth for a few minutes, return, take seats, and bow their heads.

Finally I had the nerve to ask the kid in front of me, "What are we doing?"

He replied, "We are going for our first confession."

Since I had no idea what confession was, I said, "What is that?"

He looked at me as if I was going straight to hell and said in disdain, "You have to tell Father your sins."

"Whose Father?" I asked, probably louder than I thought.

By this time he was highly annoyed and shushed me up. I was getting closer and closer to my turn and was still clueless as to what was happening. As soon as he went into the booth, I knew I was next.

In desperation, I turned to the kid behind me.

"What do I say when I go in?"

He seemed much nicer and said, "Forgive me, Father, for I have sinned."

Sin? What sin? I thought.

He then started to recite something else, but this time the nun, who could sniff out trouble a mile away, gave us the evil eye. I walked into the dimly lit booth and stumbled upon the kneeler. I figured that much out and knelt down across from the mesh screen.

I could see eyes on the other side, so I immediately closed mine. It had to be okay because I noticed the nuns did it every time they prayed out loud.

I waited in silence before I bellowed the words, "Forgive me, Father, for I have sinned."

Then I waited in silence again. The priest may have been talking to me, asking me to tell the sins, but I thought he was saying some prayers. Then I felt the vibration of a faint knock from the other side. I took it as my sign to leave, scurried off the kneeler in a matter of seconds, and was out of there.

I walked back to my seat, probably much faster than what was considered pious, and copied what everyone else had done. My heart was hammering as I waited for the nun—whose large girth under her flowing black tent could have leveled me—to haul me back to the booth and demand I repent. It seemed like an eternity until she declared that class was dismissed and I was home free.

That Sunday, dressed in my new shirt and tie, I received my First Holy Communion with the rest of my class. After Mass, the nun smiled for the first time through green teeth and declared, "Boys and girls, now Jesus is in your heart." It had to be true. After all, she was a nun. It was at least a year later before I learned that in confession I was to tell the priest what I had done wrong, the things that were against the Ten Commandments. The only commandment I knew was, "Thou shall not kill," and since I hadn't committed that one, I had no reason to return. I had to hope that the occasional insect I stomped on did not count and that God had given me a free pass on my first try.

This was my earliest impression of organized religion and although it left me feeling unsettled, I felt no compelling sense that religion had anything to do with my connection to a divine source or the God I felt was in me. The space where I felt a sense of spirit was uplifting. It did not squeeze me into a set of rules that would have landed me in heaven or hell. I never second-guessed how it got there or that it wanted anything of me, it just felt right.

In many ways, I was bothered by the traditional view of an almighty God that would take my brother away and not give me hearing like most of the population. My going to church on the appropriate holidays, like Christmas and Easter, did not further the case for traditional religion. I never made the remotest connection that what I sensed from within could possibly be this same spirit that seemed to run a tight ship on what should and shouldn't be done and proclaimed to have cornered the market on truth. Everything seemed to focus on what you were told to believe, rather than on how it made you feel. I already had enough trouble keeping up with my lessons at school, so contending with church dogma, took a backseat in importance, for better or worse.

As my physical maturation seemed to be taking a hiatus, I was equally concerned with improving my strength and athletic ability. We were having our fifth grade annual physical fitness trials involving the usual push-ups, pull-ups, and sit-ups in a two-minute period, followed by the fifty-yard dash, the quarter-mile run, and a sprint run between cones that were set up on the basketball court. Overall, the test was rigorous and we would not know our results until the awards day.

With all the background noise and excitement in the auditorium, I missed most of what took place, but picked up bits and pieces of a congratulatory pep talk from the coach. I did not hear him call my name as a recipient of the most coveted Presidential

Physical Fitness Award and the "most improved athlete." I had no idea he was talking to the student body about me until someone gave me a nudge and pointed to the stage. Before I knew it, I was making my way towards the front amidst a thundering applause. I was hesitant and surprised as I shook the coach's hand, still not quite sure of what I had received. I walked off trying to read the plaque, but by the time I was back to my seat, the applause had already died down. It was a weird experience to win something, receive a round of applause not fully understanding it was about me, and then feel elated after the fact. It was one of those moments in life when I wanted an instant replay. The surrounding sound and the scene were incongruent with one another like a bad editing job in a movie. It felt like a strikeout when, in reality, I had scored a home run.

I waited until I was home and by myself before I took off my hearing aid and went into the silent space where I decided to take my own victory lap. I acted as if I had heard every word, envisioning all the nice and encouraging things he might have said about me. I replayed coach Sherwood calling out my name; I felt the excitement and emotion that accompanied my sense of accomplishment and pride. I heard the thunder of applause over and over again. What an amazing transformation in how I felt as I reinvented the moment. Visualizing can be as—or more—gratifying than the actual event. I compensated for what I could not hear then by seeing it in my mind.

By editing the experience, I altered the impact of what got stored in my subconscious. I had the ability to amend my experience and recreate it with different eyes. I had no idea that my emotions had a profound impact on how I continued to view the world, let alone my attitude or my outlook on life. I didn't understand that while I couldn't change the past, I could at least change how I felt about it. I just simply refused to allow my most gratifying experience to go unfelt.

By the time I entered the sixth grade, I felt bigger, stronger, and more secure about myself physically, but still felt like a social misfit. I desperately yearned to fit in with my peers. It was also more apparent that with each year, I was falling more behind academically. I struggled just learning to write a sentence and understand the basic principles of grammar. It was hard enough for me to learn to converse, and now I had to write as well. I'd spent years relying on lipreading. I hadn't heard everyday language repeated, again and again. New and unfamiliar vocabulary was just a further obstacle in the growing communication jungle.

I was not one to hide my frustration, especially when it came to learning. Because I was mainstreamed with my disability, I was pretty much on my own to get it or not. Most of the time, even if I heard what was being said, I worried whether I had heard it correctly. But I did not want the humiliation that came with admitting my ineptness with hearing and words. It became more important for me to fit in and not appear stupid or unaware.

I often found myself daydreaming rather than struggling to pay attention to the teacher. Many of my happiest moments had already been experienced in my world of make-believe, inadvertently anchoring the belief that if I could conceive it in my mind, it was a part of my reality. However, I did not limit this practice to conceiving peaceful solutions. I also played out fights in my mind with those who ignored or teased me. Of course, I always emerged as the victor in those mental bouts, but this only fueled my fears and my perception that I needed more protection. This self-created mind game worked in both directions by creating negative outcomes whether I had intended them or not. The more I put my attention on a thought, the more I manifested it in my reality.

The downside of boosting my self-confidence through fantasy was that I sometimes lacked the judgment to hold back. I was absolutely terrified of thunder and lightning storms, which did not correlate with my newly formed macho persona. One afternoon after school, while satisfying my ferocious appetite with a peanut butter sandwich, I noticed it was getting oddly dark outside. Mom had just left to go to the grocery store. I walked through the kitchen and approached the front screen door. In a matter of seconds, torrential rain poured from the sky, followed by the roar of thunder. I could see my little sister Tracy running around the front lawn, frantically trying to pick up her toys.

"Tracy, get in here!" I yelled.

She ignored me. By this time, lightening was flashing everywhere. It was useless for me to yell to her. She was not coming in until she found her doll. I took off my hearing aid so I wouldn't drench the only connection I had with my outside world, and I made a mad dash out the door. Freshly broken branches and other debris were flying across the front lawn and into the street. I managed to get Tracy safely back inside, still throwing a hissy fit about her doll. She was having none of it and made a break for the front door. The storm was getting worse and I feared the lightening would strike us dead if we left the house.

"Tracy, stop! I will go. Get in the house now!"

I could barely see ahead. The water was gushing down so hard it felt like a thousand darts pinging on my skin, but a mad rush of adrenaline pumped through me. The doll was nowhere in sight. As I turned away to call it quits, I saw her crying in front of the door.

"Go back inside!" I yelled.

I ran further, knowing it could have been swept away from where she was playing and carried into the already flooded road. Suddenly I felt that the lightening was chasing me in relentless pursuit, like a wild animal desperate to seize its prey. I ran faster, determined to outsmart it.

And then, for no reason, I stopped and stared up into the sky. I did not move as rounds of lighting struck in rapid succession. I did not surrender or give in an inch. Transfixed in the middle of the street, with water covering my shoes, I defied lightening to strike me. I stared boldly into the sky for what seemed like an eternity, daring the forces of nature to break my stance. In those steadfast moments, I felt my fear pale and wash over me, leave my body, and run off me, into the street and down the gutter that was already clogged with mud. I threw both of my fists up in the air and declared victory. I didn't run back to the house, but walked back with bold self-assurance that I had stared fear right in the eye and had said, "No more!" I felt I had conquered a fear, but the vehemence of my emotion to conquer created more need to conquer and added a new layer to my armor of invincibility.

Tracy was waiting for me just inside the door, so happy to see me that she forgot about the doll. When the sun came out, Tracy's doll was never found. The universe, in its ebbs and flows, will both take and give back and it is in this polarity where we must find our balance.

One day that same year, while watching the *Wide World of Sports*, I became absorbed with a segment on competitive rifle shooting and instantly felt it was something I could do with great precision. After badgering my parents and refusing to take no for an answer, I managed to link up with the Westport rifle shooting program. I learned how to shoot a rifle properly and learned all its safety features, as well as all the rigid guidelines of competition. I was one of the youngest shooters in the class, and I ended up taking home most of the awards.

This ability did not come just by applying my shooting skills. It was first conceived in my mind. I looked at the coveted gold trophy with a shooter positioned on the granite trophy base. With unshakable confidence, I declared to myself, "I own this!" I saw it clearly displayed in a place of honor with a light shining on it, next to my Little League trophy. I felt how proud I would feel when I accepted it and how I would smile and thank the police association that conducted the program for giving me this opportunity.

When the event began, my mind remained fixed on winning as we all set up our positions in the shooting stalls. One of the biggest challenges I encountered was the fact that there were three other stalls lined up next to each other, different shooters firing their shots intermittently. I knew to turn off my hearing aid, so I would have nothing but complete silence and total focus. Those things, coupled with my dead-centered aim would allow me to win. After I had completed all ten shots, the target was brought back in, calibrated, and scored. Ninety-eight! Whoa! I felt delirious! Not only did I win the trophy, but also earned the rank of a pro-marksman. I had envisioned the win and began with that end in mind. I had listened to that inner place of winning where imagining is believing.

One of my biggest hurdles came unexpectedly at the end of sixth grade. My mother sat me down one afternoon when I returned home from school. I knew the look on her face, the one that revealed "danger zone ahead." I needed to engage a full defense, which I had perfected through exhaustive effort. I braced for whatever had prompted the "we need to talk" look. Mom did not sugarcoat things and got right to the point.

"Mike, I have spoken with your teachers and we have agreed that it would be best for you to attend Long Lots Junior High School next year, where they have a program for students with special needs."

"You mean I will not go to Bedford with all my friends?" I said, trying not to show that my heart had died and gone stone cold.

"Yes, Mike," she said sweetly. "But, honey, you can still keep the same friends you have already made and then be able to make new ones as well."

"No," I screamed.

"No way! I will not go and don't call it special needs. Everyone knows it is a school for retards."

"Michael! I will not tolerate that kind of disrespect in this house. Do you understand?"

"I mean it, Mom. Don't do this to me!"

"It has already been done and that is that. We know what is best for you and although I can see it upsets you now, it will work out just fine."

I knew my determination and boldness had come from her and she was not backing down. But then again, neither was I.

"Mom, you don't get it. I am not going."

I stomped out of the room, fighting back tears and slamming every door behind me. She knew better than to follow me.

I felt totally powerless, despite my vehement protest. The first strike had been leaving my neighborhood friends in Michigan and moving to Connecticut, not to mention repeating first grade. Strike two had been the devastating loss of my brother, which had been like a fastball to the head. Then to be pitched this third strike, which rendered me "special needs" and took me from my friends, how could it not be a strike out? It just wasn't fair. My angry tears, now totally out of control, stung my face. Mom came to my room an hour later and knocked on my door. I did not answer. When she walked in the room and started to speak, I pulled off my hearing aid as a combative gesture, turned my back on her, and waited for her to leave the room. This was my unspoken declaration of war.

I knew better than to engage Dad because he would always uphold what Mom decreed and then I would have two parents to battle. And Mom never went to Dad. She preferred autonomy in these matters and was adept at holding her ground with all the Gannon boys. My next strategy was to inform her that I was going to talk to my teachers and convince them, just as I had with the music class. I would speak my truth and get them on my side.

She answered firmly, "Fine, Mike, if that is what you wish to do. But it is not negotiable and you will only upset yourself further."

I knew she meant it, but I was not ready to throw in the towel yet.

"Do you think, Mom, that I am not good enough? Is that it?"

I knew that would get her, but she did not even flinch. Then I hit below the belt.

"Why did all of this happen to our family Mom? Matt died. Tracy is deaf and so am I." I knew not to attack Brian so I said, "So what is wrong with Doug? Tell me Mom, is he handicapped too?"

I had not meant it. I just wanted to strike back at her. It was as if I slapped her in the face.

"Mike," she said in a hurtful and defeated tone, "Doug is retarded."

I literally collapsed into a breathless pause. I was stunned. I'd had no idea. I wanted to take it back and pretend I had never asked the question or heard what she had said, but it was too late.

"I'm sorry, Mom. I am really sorry."

I had crushed her in my own war. I had hurt her in a way she did not deserve and I felt instant shame.

It was the last time I ever fought about the new school. On the first day of seventh grade, I left friends behind. Already I had coped with loss. This time would be no different. I secretly vowed to return to Bedford for eighth grade. For me, there was always a way. If I couldn't go through the front door, I would try the back. I was first in line to make things happen. I refused to feel vulnerable.

Seventh grade was a long and lonely year for me. I did not make many new friends but, rather, withdrew into a space of isolation. I understood the various struggles and frustrations of my classmates and always had a soft spot in my heart for them, but did not connect with their disabilities. Interestingly enough, there was another hearing-impaired boy in class, but I did not befriend him. One of my few friends was a student named Brian who had diabetes and often missed school. We were both friends with a paraplegic boy who had a great sense of humor. He made me laugh and forget, for a short time, that this was a totally new and different place of learning.

At night, I often imagined I was in class at Bedford Junior High with my friends, where I felt I belonged, but each school morning I returned to the disheartening reality of Long Lots. There was one saving grace. I loved all my teachers, especially my old tutor from third grade, Mr. Tunick.

At this point, I became obsessed with my quest for self-improvement. I felt that not being able to make it in the hearing world rendered me not good enough. I was astonished that there were books that actually taught you to improve yourself and I was determined to read whatever I could to help me along the way. Self-help books were becoming popular and I would save all my allowance to buy what promised to be my salvation. I also found my first copy of *Muscle and Fitness* magazine with pictures of Arnold Schwarzenegger. I became fascinated with his physical achievements and idolized his accomplishments. I was only twelve years old, but if he could overcome a language barrier, I could make it with a hearing loss. I identified with his success and modeled his routines. I found refuge in weight lifting and began a strenuous workout program that I adhered to as a way of life. I would build a protective wall with my body where no one could harm me or take advantage of me again.

Even with my determination to be strong, it was still not enough. I knew, on some level, that there was something more waiting to be discovered, so I searched relentlessly for books that held the secret. Of course there was none. I was already good enough. I just didn't know it.

My year at Long Lots had given me a miracle of a very different kind, which cannot be described, only felt. It gave me a new perspective on Matt. I would not have wanted him to suffer any more than he already had in his abbreviated physical embodiment. God had not wanted that for him. He'd had a far better game plan to execute. Intuitively, I knew that this better game plan had meant freedom from the physical world. For the first time in the four years since Mattie's death, I left behind the anger I'd felt about him being gone. I closed that door. I left Long Lots after one year, as I had promised myself. Mom had her way and now it was my turn. I was worth the fight.

I could cope with adversity with a much more positive attitude. I could do things my own way or I could accept help. I found that my choice would change the outcome of the game, if only in my thoughts.

THE CHEESE STANDS ALONE

chapter 6

Gandhi may have been right about being the change we want
to see in the world, but I hadn't yet been exposed to that
idea when I returned to Bedford Junior High for the eighth grade.
Despite the additional assistance, tutoring, and wonderful support
of my teachers at Long Lots, I wanted to block out the experience
and move on from where I'd left off at Bedford.

How different we all might be if, from the time we first began to assimilate thoughts, we were reinforced with the knowledge
that our thoughts—be they positive or negative—attract more of
the same, over and over. Especially when we are young, most of us
are conditioned to take on the beliefs of our parents. We seem to
instinctively repeat behavior without paying attention to the result.
As they begin to form a sense of self separate from others, two-year-
olds use the word "no." Wouldn't it be wonderful if they identified
with the inclusiveness of "yes" instead of the separation of "no"?

Observe any three-year-old conjuring up the most
extraordinary imaginary tale and the enthusiasm with which the

tale is met. Then notice how quickly the same skill at creating with their imagination is squelched, as they get older. Our belief system about what is true versus what is make-believe encourages children to suppress imagination. What a child thinks and feels will ultimately determine who they become. Parents are influencers, but they do not choose the outcome. When we come from a place of lack in our thoughts and feelings, we get back more lack. And many of us are unaware of that simple equation.

When we fuel our own resistance to change, like I did by hating going to a new school without my friends, we unknowingly weaken the outcome. Many of our beliefs, sold to us as being in our best interests, program us not to stray too far away from the norm. We become conditioned like pack animals, carrying our loads and plodding through life as accepted members of the collective "we."

I battled to be accepted as one of the herd but without Gandhi's wisdom to guide me, I was not the change I wished to create. The change did not start with them accepting me; it started with me accepting me.

My year at Long Lots had shown me how much academic content I had already missed, as well as how little I really understood in a typical verbal exchange. Once I left Long Lots—an environment of acceptance and the assurance that I understood what was being said—I knew I was on my own to get it or not. Most of the time, it was easier to nod in recognition rather than to painstakingly make sense of what was actually said. I had to surrender to the reality that I would miss what was said or drive everyone else crazy by asking them to repeat themselves. One of my speech therapy teachers suggested I work on becoming a better observer as

I socialized with my peers. I attempted to remain incognito while I zeroed in on the art of idle chitchat between classes.

The "if only" mantras sped through my mind on a fast track to nowhere. "If only" I had something interesting to say, something in common with them. "If only" I could converse with them and hear what they said back. Then I could grow up with them as a part of their world, rather than just pretending to be one of them. I searched for a way to understand what it was like to be one of my peers, instead of the deaf kid. My belief that I had to do more, be more, or simply try harder turned healthy determination into masked resentment. What I most wanted after my yearlong absence was a homecoming with known faces who would welcome me back and reassure me that this was where I really belonged.

This sense of myself and my place in the world stood in stark contrast to my Long Lots experience. Despite the perception by the outside world that Long Lots fostered individuality and was a place where disabled students could grow and learn, most of us there knew one thing: we were not like those outside the school's walls. None of us tried to fit in with one another; it was almost an unspoken communal understanding. We held little in common other than the same physical location. None of us were in danger of becoming sheep. I had no idea what it was like to have cerebral palsy, any more than another classmate knew what it was like to be deaf.

Sometimes the dynamics between students were impossibly difficult and complex, as they were between me and a girl I really liked. We might have been good friends had there not be one persistent barrier: she stuttered terribly. Coupled with my deafness, it was *Saturday Night Live* at its best.

It was impossible for me to decipher the convulsive tremor of her lips as she rapidly repeated the first syllable of each word, desperately trying to impart her message. She wore braces that turned her mouth into a garden hose, the contents of which I tried not to swab from my face. With great persistence, she refused to give up until she had imparted her message—one I seldom understood. So as not to insult my deafness, she would start over again. On the second round, I would try to let her know, early on, that I could not understand. This only served to mount her frustration to be heard and mine to put an end to the circuitous communication. I discerned, very quickly, that if I gave any hint that I had not heard her, we were in for another round.

But in the end, I also had empathy for others and held the deepest respect and esteem for my teachers. Still, it was not enough. My own stubborn resistance chipped away at my self-confidence and fueled my uncompromising resolve to be back in the mainstream.

I greeted my old friends with the unruly excitement of a puppy reunited with his littermates, but for the most part, I was disappointed. It seemed like no one, not even my best friend Lee, returned my enthusiasm. I felt like an outsider among my old friends. At times, I sensed they turned and changed direction when they saw me coming. At other times, they gave me the brush-off by saying, "Hey, I will give you a call," and then never calling. They probably remembered that it was a nightmare to converse with me on the telephone. There seemed to be a different societal milieu that no longer included me. I had not changed, so why had they? I felt singled out more by avoidance than anything else.

It reminded me of an old standby game we had played in elementary school called "The Farmer in the Dell." One person was designated the farmer and he stood in the middle of a circle while the others danced around him and sang the song, "The Farmer in the Dell." At the end of the first verse, the farmer chose a wife. At the end of the second verse, the farmer chose a child. This continued on through the song's verses until the last verse. I had hated it and never understood the cruelty of choosing one person over another. I was often the last one picked and would cringe as my fellow classmates danced around me, shrieking, "The cheese stands alone, the cheese stands alone, hi-ho the derry-o, the cheese stands alone." It reminded me that I was unlike them, even though it was just a game. I had to build my own armor of protection. I had to learn to shrug it off.

"Truth hands you the comb after you have lost your hair," says an old Chinese proverb. My classmates had not changed in how they felt about me. I had changed in how I felt about me. I had spent a full year dreaming of coming back to my old school and concentrating on making that happen, but it was not a positive, uplifting focus. It had been shadowed by my feelings of lack. Without knowing how or why, I had energized and attracted into my life what I had not wanted.

I had never heard of the law of attraction at the time and even if I had, I might have found it confusing. *You get what you focus your attention on.* That "law" does not differentiate between what you want and don't want. It simply states that you get what you focus on—whether or not it is what you want.

I wanted to be back with my friends at Bedford, not just because they were my friends, but also because they gave me a stamp of approval, a sense of belonging. That sounded like a positive move for me, but my thoughts and feelings came from feeling badly about myself. On the surface, it felt like a good thing to want to be with friends, to want to be in a situation where I could learn how to function. I felt I could learn how to function best in the real world of hearing people. I did not need to be defined as disabled.

But here was the glitch. My reaction to Long Lots had fostered the feeling that I did not belong in that school, which recreated more of that same experience of "not belonging" when I returned to Bedford. The underlying feeling of lack attracted more lack. We create our reality in whatever form of thinking and feeling we put out, whether we intend it or not, and I created a reality I had not intended.

My daily routine entailed the familiar activities of going home, working out with weights, and diligently wading through my homework in the evening. I said good night before going to bed and good morning when I got up, then repeated the same activities one more time. Even my brother Brian ignored me most of the time, making no attempt to conceal the fact that spending time with me was torture. He was smart, popular, and extremely good-looking. He appeared to feel a greater burden to be successful because he was the only one of us born without a disability. Dad had expectations that he make a name for the family with his athletic achievements.

Besides, who was I to blame him or anyone else for not wanting me around? I felt the same annoyance hanging around Doug. I had little tolerance for provocation. He loved to chew his food into a nasty mush, then turn to me at the dinner table and open his choppers wide to see what kind of reaction he could invoke. It seemed that he found his niche in the family dynamics through disruptive behavior and the sense of satisfaction at being able to get a rise out of someone.

The only time I ever declared in public that Doug was retarded was when I saw he was engaging in a heated argument with older guys. I assumed they did not know he was retarded and I was right. They backed off instantly and never bothered him again, even though his taunting was an ongoing annoyance. From my vantage point, he did not appear to be mentally challenged like some of the kids at Long Lots, just oddly disturbed.

One of the ways I could relate to Brian was through his love of sports. He was a tremendous athlete and I learned from his example. I also loved the sense of inclusiveness that being on a team fostered, so one of the first things I decided to do when I returned to Bedford was to try out for the wrestling team. I was still fairly small for my age and only qualified for the lightest weight category, which was called the "bantam" class. This word, which had originally meant "a small domestic fowl," had, over time, also come to describe someone small and, like the bantam rooster, rather combative in nature. Most disliked the name and the implication, but I remembered seeing two chickens fight while visiting my grandparent's farm. They attacked each other with such vigor and tenacity that I was impressed by their agility and staying power.

There were three other teammates in my weight class vying for the starting spot. I knew I was the strongest contender, but because my actual technique needed refinement, I was redshirted for the season. It was not a setback for me. I could still practice as a backup and enjoy the camaraderie of the team. I remained committed to becoming a starter when I returned the following year.

As much as I enjoyed and sought the company of others, I still relished my time alone. I secretly held on to my childhood belief that the superheroes of my dreams were really me. It was my form of self-love, my security blanket shielding me from the space where disappointment and hurt shattered imagination. This extraordinary place—which most would call my mind—held no limitation. I triumphantly defeated the enemy and never doubted or failed to overcome any impediment that I could not slay. But it was not always a battleground. I would attune my mind to a space I called the "God sound." It was peaceful and uplifting, but I never admitted to a soul that that I had heard music from as early as I could remember. It was so unlike the harsh clatter of music jamming the junior high school auditorium. It awakened my senses in such a profound way that I could never describe it. My ears were not the receiving mechanisms of the sound and there were no words or musical notations to remember.

Just as we give life to our physical body by unconsciously inhaling and exhaling, this formless music, this silent orchestration, gave breath to my inner self. That inner self was completely peaceful and all I would ever need to sustain it was already contained within me. But as a teenager, I did not fully comprehend that it was love that comprised that inner peace, that love surrounded me no matter what I did or where I was. I didn't yet know that when we listen with our hearts rather than our ears, it is all that we ever need.

I'd improved my wrestling skills and improved my physical conditioning by the next wrestling season and had every intention of making the team. Only one glitch remained when it got down to the final cut. My opponent was a friend. Was it worth the competition? These were the finals and I had to detach or hand over the victory. The match was intense. We were even on points and I almost had him pinned. Ultimately, I had to beat him on points—and I did.

I was the new starter but, as I had suspected, it took a toll on our friendship. It was hard for me to accept that winning meant naming a loser. I also learned that when parents and coaches tell you, "It's not winning or losing that matters, it's how you play the game," they don't really mean it.

The day of my first match, the gymnasium was packed. Lee and some of my other friends had come to support me, but what really inspired me was the cute blonde I spotted in the bleachers. I had seen her a few times and all it took was her smile to open my heart. I hadn't thought much about the high school dating psychodrama, I was just happy with the notion that she might have come to see me in the match. Losing was no longer an option, which added a new dimension to my performance. I took off my hearing aid in order to wear the protective headgear and the abrupt silence propelled me inward to that place where anything was possible. I did not need the final bell that signified the end of the match. I had won and the referee raised my arm above my head acknowledging me as the winner. I walked off the mat never hearing the uproarious sound of cheers from my friends or the blonde. I needed no high performance ears to hear the crowd's jubilation or to feel my own. I had already won before the match began.

The school's "Sadie Hawkins" dance would be my next opportunity to crank up my extracurricular life and ditch the social anxiety for good. I was determined to ride out the fear no matter what happened and since I could go stag, not going was not an option. Unfortunately, I did not understand the theme or the accompanying dress for the event. The first person I encountered was decked out in full hillbilly regalia, as were my other classmates, and there I stood in my finest Sunday suit looking like the preacher's kid. I hated when I missed pertinent information that reduced me to looking and feeling ridiculous.

Some jerk asked me if I was a "city slicker" and bingo, I used it as my introductory line the rest of the night. Not wearing jacked up jeans and a red flannel shirt did give me the distinct advantage of looking rather suave within a sea of country boys. In deference to the party theme, I did take a piece of hay from the set design and used it as a toothpick.

The school cafeteria was packed with students. I could not understand a thing above the dull roar of commingled voices bantering back and forth at breakneck speed. Someone would start and finish a sentence before I even got a chance to figure out who was speaking. And the possibility that I would actually comprehend what was said was not likely. The music was loud and vibrated in sync with nothing familiar. The unadulterated chaos felt like a death chant telling me the end was imminent. I decided to go home.

I circumnavigated my way through a horde of sweating bodies writhing to music that hurt my ears. I noticed that the exit was blocked by a group of cocky guys in my class. I did not want to interact with them, so I stood nearby, pretending to admire the makeshift poster that read "Sadie Hawkins Dance." It was a lame maneuver, even if it did keep me from running right past them and out the door. They did not move, which meant I had to work my way back through the crowd. I so wished I could spear a pitchfork at them and send them flying in every direction. Whose idea was it, anyway, to come to this thing?

As I started to walk back across the room, there she was, my captivating blonde from the wrestling match. This was my chance to make a move. I cleared my throat to make sure my most macho voice came through. My impaired intonation, along with my changing voice, sometimes made me sound like a cross between a neutered chipmunk and one of the hit men in *The Godfather*. As I closed in on her, my eyes felt like laser beams. Then she looked back at me. That was a good sign. She was smiling and I only had a few yards to go. I could feel my guard letting down and smiled back. Then, as if someone had shouted, "Fire!" she darted totally in the opposite direction and vanished into an elusive sea of bodies and out of sight.

I was mortified. It was an outright, in-your-face, cold-blooded rejection. I turned away as quickly as she had, but in the direction of the fire exit sign that allowed me to escape unseen into the darkest night I had ever known.

Angry tears stung my cheeks and ropes of snot poured from my nose, which I wiped away with my shirtsleeve. I despised her now, when only moments ago she could have melted my heart. What could I have possibly done to elicit that kind of reaction? I kept walking steadily, not wanting to draw attention to myself from those in the cars passing by me, but I really wanted to bolt. As soon as I had gained some distance from the school, I ripped off my hearing aid in defiance and threw it to the ground. What was the use? I couldn't hear with it anyway. I didn't hear well enough to even hang out at some contrived redneck party. I clenched my fist with nothing to punch but my own chest. All of my acrimony surfaced like a bulimic expulsion. I welcomed my self-righteous voice of entitlement that had always pulled me out of alignment and into a state of dis-empowerment.

Then, as if I had plunged that same fist into a pot of boiling water and instinctively yanked it out, I screamed inwardly, "*Stop! Stop doing this to yourself!*" It did not matter what she thought about me. It did not matter what any of them thought. In that deafening silence, where I could not even hear my own breathing slow down, I felt my inner spirit gently intercede and squelch my remaining anguish.

A higher, softer vibration carried me to another place, a place of understanding. I reached down, picked my hearing aid off the ground, wiped it clean with my shirttail, and cradled it in my hand. It truly embodied the miracle that allowed me to hear and even though it was not perfect, it was all that I had. I walked with purpose back to the parking lot and waited for my dad to pick me up. I was grateful for the inner prompting that had interrupted my emotional tailspin and deadlocked my angry self-berating. I felt much better, without numbing out to what I had experienced. I chose to stop and listen for a better way out of my pain, and for the first time, I let it go.

Much later, I was able to reflect on and understand what happened that night. I had allowed my own negative mind babble and interpretation of how others thought of me to determine how I felt about myself. I then projected it on the blonde as if she were the one responsible for my pain. I was not aware that my own self-denigrating thoughts were responsible for my feelings and outburst. I had inwardly expected rejection and attracted the proof. My feelings of unworthiness had poisoned my own thoughts and created the outcome I had feared.

What transformed everything that night, even before I screamed at myself to stop, was that I tore off my hearing aid. While I had thought it was a gesture aimed at diminishing its usefulness, it was really an unconscious act of shutting down the voice of self-abuse. In the resulting silence, I disconnected from my pain-body and listened from within. That state of allowing let my voice from within guide me.

One day a few weeks later, the same blonde walked by me in the school library. She looked straight into my eyes and smiled as if to say, "You're okay." I had shifted from the place of negativity to a different energy. I had realigned myself to a higher vibration and had attracted a more positive state. The pain was not who I was. It is not my identity. My thoughts about the pain had made me unhappy. I was fortunate to discover that truth. How easily we create stories about how inferior or wrong or undeserving we are, and how easily we allow those beliefs to create a diminished future for ourselves. The gift of this understanding emerged from that night and although it was never fully understood in this light until decades later, it profoundly changed me from the inside out.

I eventually reconnected with my peers with enough buoyancy to reconsider connecting with the opposite sex, but it probably had more to do with my budding male hormones than anything else. I had learned what the "F" word meant back in the sixth grade but had dismissed the concept rather than delve into what appeared to be forbidden territory.

My dad had referred to "the birds and the bees" once or twice, but with my hearing loss, it had become a convoluted scenario in which the birds and bees had babies together. Both parents had modestly suggested that if either Brian or I wanted to know about sex, we could come to them. Dad had strategically placed the classic book, *Everything You Always Wanted to Know About Sex *But Were Afraid to Ask* on the top shelf of the family library.

As for any risqué talk among my male friends, this was not exactly material you dared repeat ten times for the deaf kid. I was totally clueless. That was the truth of it. Sex education class in eighth grade was the deal clincher. Nothing like a graphic rendition of male and female sexual parts projected onto a six-foot screen to propel one into pubescent shock. With visual aids, I did learn enough to make sense of the basics. Fortunately I kept enough to myself for my basic naiveté to remain private. It turned out that Dad had done all right by buying that book. It proved useful. And judging from its earmarked pages, I was not the only Gannon who had visited its contents more than once.

My matriculation back into mainstream education had not been a mistake. I was learning more than any curriculum could offer. I was less frustrated and reactive when things did not go my way. I took total advantage of turning off my hearing aid. I could tune out an entire marching band with one flick of the switch and the ability to do that gave me the freedom to explore an entire dimension of my life that I did not have a word to describe. Perhaps it was my sixth sense. It was a place where vision overcame reality and the possibilities were endless. It made me feel in control and powerful, not in a negative, ego driven way, but in a way that was grounded in a developing trust in my own internal knowing. Perhaps our collective belief system has shifted away from our being "creators," deferring that power to some higher power that is in charge of our universe, and I reclaimed my birthright as a creative being. I stopped limiting myself by the stories I told myself and stepped into my ability to go inside and hear what was true for me. How did I "hear" without hearing? I just did.

Although my inner space of knowing made me feel I was in charge of my future, clearly I was not. One evening late in the spring of 1975, I came home late from school and entered the house via the screen porch. Dad was home earlier than usual. Mom was sitting across from Dad with her arms folded over her chest in protective mode, and the expression on her face warned of an impending storm. Dad was in persuasion mode, something I could tell from the way he leaned forward in a posture of authority. They continued the discussion, unaware of my presence.

From what I could glean, Dad had received an unexpected but tremendous promotion to vice-president of marketing. It meant relocating our family to a new area, but it also meant a substantial salary increase. He promised a new house, with new neighbors and friends, but Mom was having none of it. She loved Connecticut, especially Westport, where she was surrounded by her close friends. There were good schools for her children and she had a lifestyle she cherished. She argued that it was unfair to all of us as well because we would have to leave our friends and Brian would be forced to transfer high schools going into his senior year. To her, no promotion of any magnitude could ever make up for uprooting her family. Dad did not let up and only pushed harder. He probably could have sold air conditioners in the North Pole, and it was no wonder that he had been promoted. But he was getting nowhere with Mom.

After all the considerations were hashed over for days, and despite Mom's and Brian's strong oppositions, he finally declared, "You have to go where your job takes you." Even though we were well beyond the days of *Father Knows Best*, his decision was final.

Mom was devastated and Brian flatly refused to go. I, on the other hand, thought it sounded like a good change and I was proud of my willingness to adapt. I would be changing to a new high school anyway and I felt I would have a new beginning. I decided to like it and kept my opinions to myself.

The school year had finally come to a close and our entire class looked forward to the traditional year-end party. I caught up with some of the guys, knowing it would be the last time I was ever in school with them. The outdoor atrium was decorated in dim lights, which made it difficult for me to have a conversation. But, in truth, I didn't know what to say. Bidding a final good-bye with a "have a nice life" finality seemed unnecessarily awkward to me. I walked back into the school, gazed back at the party, took one last look at all of their faces, and silently exited Bedford for the very last time.

I did not resist; I was not fearful. I was not simply giving up something old and familiar. Rather, I had been given the opportunity to experience something new. Had I not made the tumultuous transition from elementary school to Long Lots and then back to Bedford, I would never have accepted what the unknown could hold for me, or the peace of surrendering to what was clearly out of my hands. I opened to this consciousness without opposition and allowed a higher power from within to show me the way.

By midsummer, we were the new residents of Great Falls, Virginia. The day we arrived at the cul-de-sac our new home sat in, I felt a new surge of energy. Sadly, I couldn't say the same for Mom. She looked and felt as if her world had been whisked from under her. Dad was his usual workaholic self, which really did not matter because Mom was beyond being appeased. Just when she had seemed to be back on her feet after the long depression that consumed her when Mattie died, she slumped back into a familiar place of vacancy.

Brian refused to adjust. Within weeks, and after many late night fights, he returned to Westport to live with family friends and finish high school. As I watched my brother walk out the door, I knew it meant seeing him less for the rest of my life—just like I knew that the day Mattie left, he was never coming home.

Doug, Tracy, and I had quickly made some new friends in the neighborhood and adjusted well to our new schools. Langley High School ranked as one of the top five public schools in the nation. As my high school years unfolded, I made a great social transition and really started to feel part of things that I enjoyed. Maybe I had instinctively stopped judging my circumstances and cleared the slate so I could start over with fresh new energy. I knew little about the psychology of emotion, just that I was feeling a new aliveness on the inside. I stopped trying to argue with the reality of "what is," especially if I could not change it. What was true was that we were living where and how we were. I was determined to make the best of it.

What good was it to get all worked up about something I could not alter? A classmate told me she could understand how hard it must be to be deaf and have people make fun of me because people made fun of her for being overweight. At first I thought it was no comparison because her condition would change if she stopped wolfing down doughnuts from the vending machines. I did not have any options; I would be deaf no matter what I did. Then I realized the reality of "what is." In the very moment that she reached out to me, she was stuck with her body the way it was, and so her comparison was valid.

I later told my mom that it made no sense for her to continue to be unhappy about the move because the reality of it was that she was in Great Falls and being unhappy would do nothing to change that. She became angry with the comment and acted hurt that I had not validated her pain. Her strong identification with the pain of leaving her past connections made her sad, not the new house, beautiful surroundings, and new people. So why was she reacting to her new setting as if they were the problem? The house was amazing, the schools the best, and the neighbors friendly and engaging. Why were her memories so much more real for her than her present reality that she refused to open a new door? I did not see how buying a ticket to her pity party helped her. Mom, who always tried to remain open and understanding, was my first naysayer, so I was not off to a rousing start with my new thoughts about acceptance.

With my inexplicable dose of self-confidence and new acceptance, I decided it was time to date. I asked out a very attractive and nice girl name Gloria. Neither of us had exchanged a word, only an occasional glance and a smile or two. She was blessed with long silky brown hair and a heartwarming smile—not to mention a killer body.

I skipped the pretense of small talk or getting to know her and blatantly asked, "Would you like to go out sometime?"

She was either too shocked by my abrupt approach or as happy as me to dispense with the formalities. Her answer was "Sure!"

We agreed to the Friday night standby of going to a movie, the safest bet for a first. As I stood before her doorbell, the butterflies in my stomach sent me into total brain freeze. Amid the long moments of excruciating silence, we barely managed to exchange the usual niceties before we arrived at the theater and parked. With my best gentlemanly behavior, I opened my door and started to go around the back of the car to open hers. In a split second she was out of the car and had totally vanished. I stood there for a moment, stunned. She was out of sight. I did not want to yell out her name, as if summoning the family dog, so I waited a second and continued to move around to her side of the car. Suddenly she popped up like one those funny little clowns you see springing out of a can.

I was bewildered, especially when the first words out of her mouth were, "Can you take me home?"

What! I thought. I felt baffled, and had no idea what to say, so I just said, "All right," and we both got back into the car. I looked over to her and said, "Are you okay?"

"I'm not feeling too well," she replied.

Within a minute or so I realized that although my ears had betrayed me, my sense of smell was compensating for them. When she opened the door and disappeared at the theater, I had not heard the retching on the other side of the car. She had evidently crouched down and vomited on the parking lot pavement. However, while in this compromising position she did not miss her shoes and the smell permeated what little air was left in my car. I did not want to be rude and roll down all the windows, but I was certain that I would be hurling too if I did not get her home—and fast.

I really felt bad for her, but I was more than happy to bid her a hasty farewell. At her front door, she looked at me with not an ounce of color in her face and with puke on her breath. "I'm sorry," she said, and quickly ran inside to hug the toilet bowl instead of me.

The whole way home I thought, *Oh, gross!* I did not have the stomach for this, but thank god my ears had spared me from the trauma of *hearing* her retch. I was rattled. I had plummeted from an exuberant high to holding the record for the shortest date. Had this happened the year before, I would have taken it personally and believed that she really did not want to be with me.

I was not quick to try another one-on-one date. I was having too much fun and doing really well in school for the first time. But in my senior year, I decided that I could not leave high school without attending the prom. Besides, all my friends would be going. It did bring back the old feelings of rejection and insecurity, but I pushed through them and summoned the courage to ask a senior girl I had met from Langley.

There was dead silence when I asked her. My heart sank. She had paused way too long and then, with hesitation in her voice, she asked if she could let me know. A stinging slap, and I had not even gotten past "go." Even though she called me a few days later and said yes, my antennas were signaling trouble.

My buddy Rob and I arranged a limo and we converged at my house for picture taking. The sun was sinking as we literally rolled off into the sunset for what would be my first and last prom. Laura looked beautiful and I was totally enamored. She wore a beautiful blue, silky long dress, which was accented by her deep tan and shimmering brunette hair, loosely pulled back. We arrived at our destination in Crystal City and I was ready for the ride to be over so I could converse with her face-to-face instead of straining to decipher the conversation.

Laura moved quickly to her entourage of friends and ignored me as I politely stood by her side until she finished. I felt left out, but dismissed it as a fluke. We headed for the outdoor patio after about ten minutes. Even though the night was hot and humid, we would at least be alone at a table for two. I felt relaxed and now it was my time to shine. No more than five minutes had passed when she asked me if she could be excused for a few minutes.

"Oh, okay, sure!" I said.

It was two hours later before she finally reappeared. In the interim, after an hour of sitting at the table expecting her to reappear at any moment, I had started looking for her and even asked another girl to check the bathroom in case she was sick.

Then, as if nothing had happened, she walked right up to me and said, "Hi." I asked if she was okay and she responded, "I'm fine," with a "drop it" air of aloofness.

Well, this was another first. I had been stood up by my prom date at the prom. Thank god it was time to leave and although we sat next to each other on the way home, I did not say a word. We arrived at her house and she exited the car without me.

"Thanks for inviting me," she chirped.

"You're welcome, Laura," I answered in a highly sarcastic tone as she trotted off into her house.

She had used me to go to the prom with the intention of making her ex-boyfriend jealous. Apparently they did get together that night, but in the end, he broke her heart. This time the humiliation smacked her in the face.

It was no mistake we had attracted each other. I mostly cared about not leaving high school without a prom date and she wanted to go with someone else. We each had a hidden agenda, so the outcome was clearly our own handiwork.

I had done well enough at Langley High School to be accepted at three good colleges. I had the typical jitters about leaving the nest, but did not question how I would handle a rigorous academic program, not to mention the competitive job market that awaited me after college. Part of it was having learned to condition my mind against buying into fear. I shut out any voice that told me I could not do something and I tried to block out extraneous mind chatter that might create obstacles. I recognized some things were harder than others, but so what? That didn't mean I couldn't do them. It was not that I was devoid of resistance, I was just aware of how the mind could run away with a thought and transform it into a much bigger deal.

Someone once asked me how I could have a driver's license and be deaf. My response was, "I can see."

"Well, what if someone honks at you to get out of the way, or an ambulance or police officer comes from behind and you don't hear the siren?"

"Well, I suppose I don't move out of the way," I calmly replied. I refused to buy into the potential drama of the question; I refused to allow my thoughts to reinforce his concerns. Once I did not buy into the fear implied by the question, the matter was dropped. His fear did not become a part of my story. I did not invite it in. I was not knowingly practicing the law of attraction or any other mental conditioning, but what I did not hear, understand, or believe did not happen because I did not consider it in my thoughts. When I was told I could not do something, I refused to believe it or feel that it might be true.

I was very methodical in the selection process of choosing the right college and personally visited each of them before my final decision. The first school looked perfect on paper but did not have the right feel from the moment I arrived. I was very much in tune with how my body reacted to my environment and rarely analytical about what it meant. It was a feeling I learned to trust that could stand alone without the words to describe it. I knew it instantly and was able to follow my instincts without hesitation or a sense of uncertainty. The second school felt much better in comparison, but I had applied there as a safety net. I did not feel it was as good academically and deemed I would be selling myself short if I attended that college.

The third, a college for the hearing-impaired, seemed totally not me, but it would also be my greatest stretch. I had never been with other hearing-impaired people, apart from Tracy. Also I had never learned signing as a way of communicating. What was I thinking? I flew to Rochester, New York, and drove to the campus of The National Technical Institute for the Deaf to give it a fair shake. Maybe this was meant to be my four-year reprieve from the stress of communicating in the hearing world.

Prior to my visit, I did not realize that N.T.I.D. was a division of the Rochester Institute of Technology and shared the same campus with hearing students. I could still keep my foot in the door in the hearing world, pledge a fraternity, and have the academic benefit of a supportive curriculum for the deaf. This was it!

I enrolled in the least likely school, in the department of electrical and mechanical engineering. I always excelled in math and technology, fascinated with the then emerging field of computers. My excitement flew me as high as the aircraft that returned me home.

I graduated from the class of '78 with a tassel throwing celebration like no other at Constitution Hall, in Washington,

DC. I had not only survived, I had thrived! It also helped that I was no longer a skinny boy, 4 ft. 9 in. tall, but 6 ft. without shoes and a solid, muscular physique.

As I graduated, I realized that I had missed the most important thing in that childhood game, "The Farmer in the Dell." The rules actually stated that the kid who ends up being "the cheese who stands alone," automatically gets to be the leader (the farmer) in the next round. I was ready.

As they say at the opening of every Olympics, "Let the games begin."

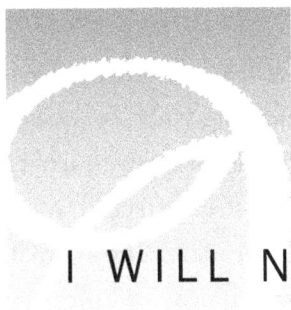

I WILL NOT HEAR YOU!

chapter 7

Months after my graduation, I methodically removed my high school diploma from its scrolled encasement so as not to bend the faux parchment filigreed edges. I stared at it in disbelief. I wanted to frame it in a bright gold wooden frame with expensive double-edge matting and proudly display it. I felt reluctant and somewhat embarrassed to expose how proud I felt of this milestone, especially when it did not seem like any big deal for most of my college bound buddies.

Intermingled with my feelings of accomplishment, I also felt an element of pretense and the apprehension of living on the edge. Much of what had been taught verbally, I really did not fully understand. Therefore, I depended on how well I performed on tests and how much I could count on studying my textbooks to learn what I needed. I had refined the art of looking as if I understood with an insightful nod. Acting "as if," even though it temporarily misrepresented my state of knowingness, usually bought me the time to figure things out.

I loved the mantra from one of my self-help books, "Fake it until you make it." It became my most validating voice as I stayed under the radar of discovery. I learned to disregard my teachers' insistence that I ask for clarification if I did not understand. Most of what I heard did not make enough sense for me to know which question to ask. If I said, "I did not understand, hear, or otherwise comprehend, a single, solitary word you just said," what then? How long would it take for the instructor to cry "uncle" and suggest that, in my own interests and out of respect for the other students' time, I should be moved to a special program? I had chosen to be a part of mainstream education, and I would do whatever it took to remain there.

I mentally expunged the immediate need to know as a survival mechanism. Impossibility did not exist for me and failure was not an option. I was pretty much on my own to come up with a plan consistent with my own beliefs or defer to the naysayers who insisted I yield to my limitations. My persistence won, but not without a price.

That same summer after graduation, Mom's prayers were answered and Dad was able to transfer back to the Connecticut office. Although Mom never verbalized it, I somehow felt she was symbolically returning home to Mattie and I was glad for her. Brian had been the first to leave home and we had all survived his departure, so I was good to go. Change was not frightening to me anymore.

The thought of going to college and having a roommate and a life separate from home arrived in perfect synchronicity with my evolving feelings about myself. I looked forward to a break from having to struggle to comprehend everything on my own. I was relieved I had chosen a college where I could get help and assistance because I knew my studies would get harder and engineering was a data specific field.

I had to either get it or forget it. The intent to move forward forced me to lighten the load internally. I would not outwardly allow myself to be pigeonholed by what others thought of me.

Somehow I instinctively knew that if I thought I was weak or less intelligent than others, so it would be. When we consistently believe in our inherent capabilities, we change the brain's circuitry accordingly. From the time I was a small child, my daydreams, my silent space of thought, determined who I would become. In that space, my voice was the only one that counted. I did not and would not hear the collective voice that branded me impaired. But I was growing weary of the struggle and needed a break. I was excited to see how other deaf students coped and share experiences with them. I was open to different thinking and I wanted to take it all in by experiencing things from diverse points of view.

I left a week earlier for college than most of my friends because I was required to take a crash course in signing. I didn't mind it. I had pretty good hand-eye coordination and I looked forward to mastering the art. More importantly, if I could communicate with greater proficiency, I could simplify the process of comprehending what was being taught. I was determined to excel and to prove myself, not just for me, but also for my parents. This was not my dream alone, but also their dream for me. They had allowed me to be my own person and map my own direction. I was pressuring myself to succeed; they wanted for me what I wanted for me. If I had wanted less, they would have been okay with that as well.

৪৩৪৩৪৩৪৩৪৩

I often wondered why Brian—with all his apparent talent—did not wish to go the extra mile, to aspire to anything outside his comfort zone. I could never get close enough to understand him on any level. He made certain that most of his life went unnoticed.

Leaving my little sister was like leaving a part of my heart behind. Mom called her "Little Miss Socialite" because everyone knew and liked Tracy. She appeared to put little pressure on herself to do anything but have fun. She was as adept in social situations as I was uncomfortable with them. She held the belief that she would not need to work, but would get married and have babies. Sadly, none of that happened for her. She unknowingly made herself into what she believed everyone else would love and left nothing for herself. Without self-love, personal fulfillment is elusive.

As for Doug, there was always something inaccessible and troubling about him. I had a hard time understanding why he was considered mentally challenged. To me, he seemed emotionally stuck in a very dark and disturbing place that no one spoke about. He caused nothing but disruption and turmoil and became more aggressive as he approached adolescence. Mom and Dad gave no other explanations and in their silence, we knew not to ask.

After several threatening incidents as a young adult, he was "permanently" hospitalized and then later released as a ward of the state. Once he was stabilized, he was transferred to a group home.

One time, during a visit, I asked him about the pills he was taking. He said, "This one is for the voices." Immediately I said, "What voices?" thinking maybe he could not sleep at night with multiple housemates and thin walls. He said as plain as day that they were for his schizophrenia. He told me he had started hearing voices as a young boy and they had told him to do bad things. He listened to loud, heavy metal music to drown them out. Why hadn't anyone told me? No one ever discussed this diagnosis. I needed to know why. I confronted my mother to find out.

"Just what is Doug's diagnosis, Mom?"

With a slight hesitation, she replied, "Well they really don't know. He is mildly retarded, probably dyslexic, and has high anxiety issues."

I could hear her voice tighten.

"And schizophrenic?" I said. She nodded in agreement and walked away. I later learned her mother had also been a schizophrenic. It is amazing how denial and abuse will wrap you in a cocoon of secrecy.

৪৩৪৩৪৩৪৩৪৩

It was now my turn to spread my wings. Amidst a teary good-bye, I left home, college bound and primed to begin one of the most amazing adventures of my life. I settled into my room and did not meet my roommate for a full week because he had used signing all of his life and was slated to arrive with the majority of students. The morning of our orientation, we assembled in a big auditorium and the president of our division was the first to greet us with the sign for "Good morning," which looked to me like the same hand signal used to mutely verbalize "Up yours." By the amused look on some of the other faces, I was not the only one making the correlation.

It was actually very moving to be relating to hundreds of other deaf people for the first time in my life. I had always been the exception, never the rule. What a quick immersion into a new and different culture. I was fascinated with this linguistic art of signing and astounded how it mimicked the ambiance of noise and commotion in an otherwise silent room. I was even more stunned that so few of my fellow students actually spoke out loud and was speechless, myself, at the innate beauty and flowing expressiveness of this way of communicating. They quietly conveyed a passionate emotion that almost made sound seem inadequate in comparison.

My new roommate hailed from Chicago and we instantly bonded. We stayed up late talking and getting to know one another, which I admit was somewhat tedious because he mostly signed and I spoke. He did not hear me and I did not understand him, but what else was new? It seemed like home. We could each relate to what the other was experiencing, so it eased any frustration. Within a few weeks, I realized how difficult it had been for him to leave home. He was attached to a serious girlfriend he had left behind—but not, apparently, without regrets. I felt helpless and unable to cheer him up. He refused to make the break and leave the room other than for class or a meal or two.

His despondency was contagious and I started to miss my home as well. My family was the foundation of my world and not being able to understand much of what they said was frustrating when I talked to Mom and Dad on the phone. It certainly did not alleviate the gnawing loneliness that had crept into the pit of my gut. I realized how much I had counted on them, especially for their day-to-day support. Still, I knew I could do it; I had to. It was my turn to step up to the plate.

I adapted to the curriculum quite well. It turned out to be so much easier to learn in an environment tailored to the needs of hearing-impaired students. Everything was done to accommodate our understanding. But by the end of the first semester, when some of the novelty had worn off, I actually missed sound. I found myself becoming intolerant of my classmates who refused to speak and use their voice. I was shocked at the garbled and guttural sounds of my deaf classmates whose voices were untrained. It reminded me of my many oppositional hours of speech therapy during which Mom and Dad had corrected me over and over again until I got it right. I understood how tough it was, but I never accepted the flat refusal to try. Maybe because I had been a child when I learned to talk and had no other options, for me it was never a matter of choice. I did not want to judge them. I knew how much it hurt. I fought my resistance to reliving my struggles with learning to speak audibly. I fought my own persistent resistance against hearing them, an "I will not hear you" stubborn refusal to understand them. Ironically, they did not necessarily want to hear me—a speaking deaf person— either. Many were surprised at how well I spoke, with just a slight hint of impaired intonation that might closely go unnoticed if one did not listen closely. All the years of grueling speech therapy had paid off and my lip-reading skills were impeccable.

In reality, I was not one of them. I had not grown up in a deaf culture and it was, indeed, a different way of life. I envied their peace of mind and the effortless way they communicated with each other. I noticed how they looked out for each other and the voiceless, picturesque language that moved their hearts and linked them in a world that was unfamiliar to me. I would see their frustration, but it was not my frustration. I could communicate in

87

their language of signing, but it was not my language. We attended class together and studied together. We shared meals, laughter, and the ups and downs of adjusting to college life, but I was never one of them. I was the outsider who spoke well, who did not rely on signing, who could hang around with other hearing students on campus, who had his own car, and who functioned well on the outside world.

Hopes of belonging to their culture were not even dashed, because I had no such hopes. I did not choose that type of exclusion. Had I been brought up in their world, it would have been different. But I had already overcome so much. I learned to love my fellow students, to accept them, to be with them, and to learn from them—but I could never be isolated from communicating and interacting outside this tightly knit group.

I felt I had emerged back into the hearing world when I found a fraternity on the hearing side of campus. To me it stood out like a neon sign saying "Rush Here!" So I did. But I was in for a rude awakening. I had no idea that the process would be so perversely ritualistic and, at times, degrading. When I began the pledging ordeal, something within me was beginning to change. Instead of feeling hurt or inferior, I made a clear decision to no longer hear or accept callous expressions of intolerance. I was angry and it showed. I was finished with being made to feel less than, invisible, and ashamed. I was well built and muscular, and for the first time, I decided to intimidate rather than be intimidated. I felt confident I could hold my own in a fight. I liked the feeling of physical power and I was tired of shrinking away and turning the other cheek (one of the rare morsels of wisdom I remembered from catechism). I would not dismiss the insensitivity of these so-called brothers-to-be. I would not be defined by what they thought of me and I would not tolerate abuse. I found that belonging to a fraternity was a high price to pay for friends and a social life. I always felt on the defensive.

I managed to end the school year with a 3.63 grade point average, but I also had the bitter realization that this was not the school for me, despite how well I had done academically. If I was going to succeed in the business world, if I was going to be "the somebody I chose to be," I had to plunge into the real world without a safety net. My guidance counselor pleaded with me to give it another year and insisted I was making a serious mistake. He reinforced, over and over, that I needed to learn to accept my handicap and accept the extra help that was available to me to reach my goals. *What then?* I thought. Would anyone offer me an easier road, simply because I was deaf? I knew the answer and I transferred to Virginia Polytechnic Institute (Virginia Tech), a highly regarded state university. And with my bombastic battle cry, "I will not hear you," to the legions of naysayers, I was more determined than ever to succeed.

STEPPING STONES AND STUMBLING BLOCKS

chapter 8

My decision to transfer schools was not devoid of complication. I was plunged headfirst into the lecture halls of Virginia Tech with hundreds of students. In a school population of about 25,000 there were only two profoundly deaf students. My hopes of actually hearing the lesson or being close enough to lip-read were shattered. It came as no revelation that this university was barely in the infancy stages of providing any special assistance. But then, wasn't that what I had opted for, not to be singled out or given preferential treatment?

My aspirations of being like everyone else took a spiraling nosedive the first semester of my sophomore year. I was failing almost every class. Humbly, with my tail between my legs, I sought the help of the guidance department and by my second semester, I was put in touch with several students who were willing to be my note takers. I spoke individually to my professors, not to excuse my performance, but to explain my circumstances. Most were receptive to my needs, but none offered any viable solutions other than the age-old advice to ask questions if I did not understand. It was at least a start, and I refused to be defeated.

With class notes and daily assignment instructions covered, I had a better handle on what was expected of me. I was entirely capable of reading the textbooks and doing my homework. At least now I felt more in control and not paralyzed by falling behind. I would not tolerate the feeling of vulnerability, the option of collapse or being out of control, not even when I felt paralyzed under a ton of rubble. With guts and patience, I would dig out, take a fresh breath, and move on.

The majority of hearing individuals automatically employ selective hearing to block out disruptive background noise. No such filter exists with a hearing aid and even the slightest backdrop of dissonance distorted the speech. In a crowded room or an inharmonious environment, I would deliberately cut off from sound to avoid the frustration of not being able to hear and the aggravation of auditory overload. "I will not hear you" wreaked havoc and invited psychological conundrums that I never anticipated. This purposeful act of disconnecting my hearing aid felt highly empowering to me. What an immense relief to have total silence when I wanted no outside distractions. But sometimes the lessons are in what we do not learn. I had no clue that I used my "I will not hear you" stance as a mechanism to protect myself from hurt or disapproval. I built a solid fortress that sheltered my ego. I not only pulled the plug on my aid, I unconsciously and selectively heard what suited me even when I was tuned in. I outwardly projected blame on others rather than feel my own inadequacy.

For example, if I missed something that was said in a conversation, my first reaction was often to ask the person if he was mumbling or speaking too loud, too soft, or too fast—whatever I deemed to be the problem. In other words, rather than accepting that I had not heard what was said, I instead suggested that it must have been the other person's failure to communicate clearly. I got away with it because most people are uncomfortable saying, "Maybe you didn't hear me because you're deaf." Instead, they repeated the phrase again and graciously accepted the blame I bestowed on them. If I became loud or argumentative, I would project my own raised voice onto the other person as if they were the ones yelling at me. "Why do you need to feel you have to scream at me?" I would ask when, in actuality, I was yelling at them. If they did not back down, I might say, "Sorry, I'm deaf. I was unaware my voice was so loud," leaving them to feel they had been insensitive.

After years of this ingrained pattern, a brave friend spoke up and said, "Stop playing the deaf card at my expense."

I got it!

I did not know to rectify what I failed to recognize. I had been so internally focused on my hearing in order to understand conversations or classroom teachings that I had no idea how transparent I had become in my own defensive posture. But getting it was only the first step. I attracted the circumstances to repeat the need for that learning over and over again. I had put down layers of ingrained thought patterns to prevent me from being vulnerable and those entrenched thought patterns were an impediment to change.

We are storytellers extraordinaire and justify what we tell ourselves to be true. The more I could filter out through my hearing what did not fit my version of how I interacted in the world, the more powerful I felt. But in my relationships with others, it held me a prisoner of my thinking.

We are creators of our own reality in many ways we do not intend. From infancy, we make neural connections in our brains that determine our reactions and our fears. We later react to past painful situations that are long forgotten. Those undigested events set us up to create situations that will trigger the same reactions later in life. Some of that conditioning does not support an effective way of being in this world, but without awareness and the ability to disrupt this habitual, energetic connection in the brain, we continue to replicate old issues and old ways of responding to them.

Neuroscience has shown us that our brains are subject to the influence of recurring beliefs, but they are also adaptable and able to make new connections. I often continued to respond according to old patterns, but I was also beginning to rewire some of my connections.

I also came to the realization that although I liked the conceptual aspects of engineering, I felt little passion for the work it would entail. I sensed that it would somehow isolate me from people and hold me hostage behind four walls and a desk. I methodically perused other curriculums that might spark my interest, but nothing stood out.

One night, shortly after dinner, as I walked back to my dorm with no intent other than to escape the cold, it hit me. I stopped, frozen in my tracks. I heard an inner voice coming from that childhood mind where visualization was the norm and I could create in living color. It seemed like such a long time since I had visited those places of fascination and fearlessness. I was so bogged down on the academic treadmill that I had lost touch with any feeling or notion of what I might want. I just knew I had to keep up my grade point average. That night, I dreamt I was drowning and that the only lifeboat in sight kept moving further away from me as I screamed for help. "I will not hear you," it mirrored back to me over and over. "I will not hear you."

When I woke up, I knew those words had meaning. I was no longer listening to myself, I was listening to what I thought I needed to do to keep afloat. I dressed for class knowing I would be late and sprinted across campus trying to forget the warning. I had always loved the thrill of sports and physical conditioning. I felt invigorated when I arrived, even though I could barely breathe. Standing in a cesspool of sweat, my answer was staring me in the face: exercise physiology! The thoughts came rolling in like claps of thunder: *sports medicine, nutrition, physical education. Yes! Yes! Yes! Do what you love!* That same day I headed back to the guidance department to map my course. By the end of the second semester, I was out of the woods. I had raised my grades and declared my new major in exercise physiology and human nutrition and foods.

I entered the school's first bodybuilding contest as a way of officially declaring my major. I had always held a fascination for this sport and as nutrition major, learning how to put on some extra muscle would not be that difficult. I had a few months to get in top shape and it would be a tremendous opportunity to train myself and learn to apply my experience to others.

I spent every extra minute in the gym and revamped my diet to exclude fats, limit carbohydrate intake, and up the protein. I reluctantly gave up beer. I also spent time reevaluating my plan based on results and was able to strike a balance between dieting and weight lifting. The final push entailed a very specific diet that would make me "ripped" for the competition. As the competition approached, I was confident the worst was behind me—or so I thought. Somehow, I did not understand that contestant posing routines needed to be choreographed to music. I knew a variety of posing moves and did them well, but putting them to music that I could not even hear was preposterous. Still, it was just one more hurdle to jump.

When the day of the competition arrived, I summoned all my friends to root for me. What was I thinking? I felt fairly self-assured with my body and tried not to be disturbed by the obligatory dance routine. I slathered the hideously colored fake tanning solution all over my milky-white skin and although I resembled an orange peel, it did accentuate my muscle definition. But the true test of both my self-assurance and my seriousness about the competition would be actually stepping onto the well lit beauty pageant type stage, flaunting a jewel-toned Speedo that defied any straight man's boundaries. The only thing that might have lessened this trauma would have been stepping onto the stage with an entire audience of blind people. As the houselights went down and the footlights came up, about three thousand students looked on as we paraded our flesh and flexed our muscles like cattle at a stock show auction.

None of us were prepared for the hot lights that transformed the stage into a sauna. Primed by heat and excessive perspiration, my tan dripped off into a pool of sludge around my boney bare feet. My hearing aid shorted out from the perspiration that flooded into my ears just moments before my solo performance. I went from hearing uproarious audience cheers to the stone-cold deaf reality of total silence. The blood drained from my head and my head refilled with instant panic. What now? All these grueling months of training reduced to a dead battery?

Hell no!

I made a beeline to a pair of 130-megawatt speakers that were placed close to each other at center stage, cranked them up, and moved them right next to me. At least I would feel the vibration. Five, six, seven, eight . . . the stage rocked with the blasting music. I posed in every direction like a naked baby released from his diapers. A jumbo 747-jet airliner registers 130 decibels of sound when it takes off, so you can only imagine these two speakers blaring at close range. The walls, the floors, and everyone's brain vibrated with earth-shattering intensity! The blinding stage lights shielded me from the terrorized faces and covered ears. Thank god I could not hear the groans! I finished my choreographed routine on perfect queue. But it was not over yet.

At the end of the individual competition, all of the contestants had to come back on stage and do what is called a posedown. With the music turned down, I was hardly able to follow the vibration. There I was, wildly thrusting my stuff. I kept right on going, clueless that the music had stopped and the other participants had left the stage. Some poor soul had to interrupt my solo performance and escort me off the stage. Clearly, the posedown was over. I won the title of Best Poser! My trophy should have read, "Embarrassed Beyond Belief." For those who attended the event that night, I think it is safe to say that they never forgot me!

By senior year, I needed to boost my overall grade point average because my first two semesters after the transfer had pulled down my numbers significantly. After four years of college, I had no intent to face a competitive job market without a decent GPA.

I went to every professor with one single question: "How do I get an 'A' in your course?" I obsessively grilled them for every lead. What exactly do I need to do? Study? Learn? Research?

One of my friends finally said to me, "Would you just chill out. It is great to study and have goals, but seriously, you're like a madman." At first I felt misunderstood. What was wrong with wanting something and taking it to the finish line? I could make things happen. That was my saving grace. But at what expense? Had I ever tried another approach, a more comfortable route that was not so black and white, or fixated in the "all or nothing" belief?

He was right. I was being this scholastic fanatic, as if nothing else mattered—not even my friends. I reminded myself about what had happened with the bodybuilding contest. I had given it my full attention and had cranked out the perfect physical result, but where was the simple warning that stage lights and sweat would hijack my hearing? No outcome was ever insured! Just because I shackled myself to my book bag and picked every brain I could in search of intellectual utopia, would it really insure me the grade or the job I wanted? Was it worth missing all of the enjoyment of my final year at Tech?

I decided to forego the madness and do the best I could. Every day I would visualize opening my grades and seeing 4.0. In the interim, I studied a great deal, but I also hung out with the guys at the local hot spots and participated in the usual college antics—like spring break in Ft. Lauderdale. I boldly welcomed the unexpected and just when I was not looking, I got what I least expected. It was not the 4.0 I had been imaging. It was a perfect 10. And her name was Laurie.

I was meeting a group of friends at a nearby Marriott and I was late. I noticed her as soon as I walked through the door. A captivating brunette with a mind-blowing smile was sitting across from one of my friends. She made eye contact with me before I even got to the table. I flirted back, and casually made my way to where she was sitting, and waited to be introduced. She had been beautiful from across the room, but she was even more beautiful close up. Yet she seemed to have no self-consciousness about it. I liked that.

It was difficult to talk with all the background noise, but because it was a group and no one else could really hear either, it worked out well. I was mesmerized by her and intended to act upon it. She was the sister of my friend's girlfriend and I received an immediate grapevine report that gave me reassurance that she was attracted to me too. Hallelujah! I could put any second-guessing aside. I seldom perceived the subtleties of anything auditory, but something about her voice made me melt. It had a very sensual, yet sincere, tone to it. She lived in a town less than an hour away and I was surprised to learn she was just turning nineteen and graduating from high school! She seemed so much more mature and wise to me.

I called her two days later and she accepted a date. From then on, we were hardly separated for more than a day or two. Finally, I felt what it was like to have a girlfriend. I became wholly enamored. She was everything to me and even encouraged me to keep up my studying and raise my final grade point average. I was grateful for my decision to tend to my personal life. It turned out that I could keep up with my studies *and* keep up with my personal life.

Mom, Dad, and Brian came down for my graduation and met Laurie for the first time. I was so proud and I knew they would like her. I felt complete. At last, on that sunny graduation day, I knew what it meant to belong, to be like everyone else, and to feel the tremendous sense of accomplishment my well deserved fourth quarter 4.0 provided. Even a hangover from the night before could not erase my gleaming smile. I was the first profoundly deaf student *ever* to graduate from the hallowed grounds of Virginia Tech. As we tossed our hats in the air, I heard something over the roar. In my minds ear, I could hear the shrieking on the otherwise silent campus at the National Institute for The Deaf. From the rooftops of Rochester, all the way to the rolling black hills of southern Virginia, I heard my classmates there shout, "We did it! And this time we hear you!"

I stayed for a few weeks longer to take another course in physical fitness education. Mostly I did not want to leave Laurie. She was going to Old Dominion University in the fall and, more than anything, I wanted to carry on a long-distance relationship. But we had yet to have the conversation. I could not imagine ever being without her. I went with her to Norfolk to help her settle into her apartment. As we walked along the harbor, the fog began to roll in. It began to cloak the shoreline . . . and my confidence. Laurie did not look at me, but I sensed her sorrow and hesitation. I took a deep breath. I knew we were about to engage in the inevitable discussion about our future.

"Mike, I think we both need to see other people," she said bluntly, as if the words had to be said with no softening preface.

Once she had spoken, I felt the tension leave her body and find its way to mine. I could not answer her or even speak, because speaking meant I would have to pry open my throat and free the words I wanted to say—words that would be of no help. I loved her so much.

She kept talking and nervously explaining that she was young and had her whole college experience in front of her. I never really heard the rest of what she said. *I will not hear you.*

I had a flashback of the moment my father announced that Matt had died. I experienced that helpless moment of no return and I began to shake inside. I closed my eyes and allowed myself to be taken away by the fog.

"We still can be friends," she said innocently, hoping to ease my pain.

I just nodded in agreement. It was all I could manage. Like Mattie, she would never be coming back. I knew that.

ON MY OWN

chapter 9

While many of my friends relocated back home after graduation, mostly as a matter of convenience and financial necessity, it was not even a moment's consideration for me. The northern Virginia area seemed more like home to me than Connecticut. Westport felt overly conventional and stodgy to me, like living in a pristine domestic time warp. It was no wonder that The Stepford Wives, with its male-dominated utopia, had been set in Connecticut.

I liked living adjacent to the nation's capital with its energy, seductive charm, and edgy young professional population. The time had come for me to seek an untried level of sophistication outside the familiar zaniness and local color of a college campus. I welcomed the finality of my degree. There were no more required classes and no endless hours of studying, no more scrambling for notes and no sweating through tests. For once I did not hold on to the familiarity of old friendships. I honored that other opportunities and relationships would show up in my life and elicit new beginnings. It was not that my past mattered less. Rather, what was ahead of me mattered more. I was infused with enthusiasm.

My eagerness paled after weeks of pounding the pavement in search of employment. With my money supply running near empty, I realized that I had better settle for a provisional job. The only prospect in the want ads that remotely reflected any of my aspirations was a position as assistant manager at a local Nautilus Health Club. I rationalized that an entry-level managerial post might enhance my comprehensive know-how in the operational aspects of the fitness industry.

I knew that first impressions were deal breakers. Rather than having the usual telephone communication hassle of not understanding and the predictable aggravation of repetition, I appeared in person to apply for the job. The encumbrance of my hearing aid protruding from both my ears and hair made its own declarative statement without the tiresome explanation of how I was born deaf. It was apparent I could carry on a conversation and speak clearly. They were immediately interested.

Forget the well-crafted resume or my degree from Virginia Tech in exercise physiology and nutrition. I was a warm body with all the moving parts. I could open the gym at 6:00 a.m., close it on occasion at 9:00 p.m., and work any of the seven days of the week. I could walk, talk, and pick up wet towels all at one time and be cajoled into accepting a low starting salary dressed in a slightly more upscale title. How could I not flourish? They wanted me as early as yesterday; I needed the money, and I accepted the job that day.

I fought back discouragement during the ensuing months, telling myself that I was in the preliminary stages of proving myself to the staff before assuming added responsibility. Had I really spent four grueling years of college so that I could count the chemically treated and tattered towels that were delivered each morning to the gym, inspect the exercise equipment for remnants of sweat from the night before, and ensure that the showers' drains were not clogged with hair?

My hours were varied from day to day, but by 6:00 a.m., the first onslaught of eager beavers arrived and by 7:30, these pumped up and showered professionals left for what I imagined to be their uptight and prestigious workplaces. Between 7:30 and 9:00 a.m., most of the real cardio freaks arrived. They scrimmaged over the time restraints on the equipment and complained that the hot water pressure had diminished in the shower. By 9:00 a.m., the mothers would start to trickle in with their kids in tow to take advantage of the nursery. It seemed to me more like a sanity escape for a particular group of out of shape, post-baby moms who worked out for maybe twenty minutes and then gossiped for the remaining forty. Considering the cacophony of whining, crying, screaming, and hysteria that was coming from the playroom, I could not blame them. On top of that, some child invariably worked up a full-blown temper tantrum that blended with the bilingual version of *Sesame Street* blasting in the background.

The beautiful people systematically spread themselves out during the day in order to be seen. For the female twenty-something set, long blonde straight hair, a bared midriff exposing sculpted abs, well toned legs, killer bare arms, and obviously stationary breast implants were the norm. The male "muscle heads" showed off the most when other men were looking, like dogs sniffing out their alpha status. Evenings encompassed all of the above, but had the decided perk of uncensored sexual energy and pheromones galore.

On the rare occasions when I actually spoke to clients about their workout regimes, it provided my only sense of real contribution. Mostly I perfected the role of glorified janitor and managed dribbles of perspiration, bathroom scuffles, and virile egos with precision. I did frame my bachelor of science degree and hung it over my makeshift desk as a daily reminder that they could "take this job and shove it." Within months, I did just that.

Major health clubs were just starting to surface and gain in popularity. They had not yet replaced the hard-core testosterone gyms where meatheads threw around weights and New Agers rented the back room to chant or do yoga. Personal training had not yet caught on. If one was interested in training amateur athletes, it was usually school based and required a physical education background. Breaking into the professional realm of training was also difficult. What now? Maybe I could be a nutritional consultant for Meals on Wheels or manage a school lunch program, but as a one-on-one trainer for health and fitness, I was clearly ahead of my time.

By 1984, the computer field was still in its infancy but growing rapidly. I halfheartedly reconsidered a more promising and lucrative career in computers. The bottom line was that I needed money to pay the bills and I did not wish to hear Dad's "I told you so" about the stiff competition in the DC market. I took a position selling computers with a fast growing company that claimed it would soon take over the marketplace.

My first day in the training program opened with a cruel and ironic twist. I was informed that most of the selling would be on the telephone, generating leads. *Oh great!* Even in my practice sessions, the incessant hangups were bloody when I did not understand the caller on the other end of the line. The same cruel inner playground voice squealed in my mind, *You can't hear, you are not like everybody else. Nany nany boo-boo, stick your head in do-*

do. And the most humiliating part was that these moronic sessions of me straining to sound semi-intelligent were being taped and listened to by my manager. He joined the throng of the impatient and suggested I seek employment elsewhere, while strategically trying not to mention my hearing impairment as the problem. I had to give the guy credit for his smoothness. Hightailing it out of there was enough for me.

I resurrected my ego and applied for another sales position—one with less telephone interaction. I took a job with a headhunting firm that was highly competitive in placing clientele who sought positions in the technical field. I stuck it out, but I could not escape the inevitable telephone debacle. I left this job as well, forced to accept that my communications skills were limited in this marketplace and definitively precluded telephone interaction.

During my short tenure with the headhunting firm, I at least made a good friend who recommended a four-day basic training course in personal development. He had just taken it and suggested that this would be a good way for me to take an earnest look at myself and determine my next course of action before plunging headfirst into another failure. It sounded encouraging and with no place else to turn, I signed up to take the course over the following weekend. I knew that the business world would be a self-inflicted battleground unless I opted for a serious attitude adjustment. It had been a tough start my first year out of college and I needed help.

The course began on a Thursday evening and there were over two hundred enrolled participants. The first night was about structuring our commitment to the rules, especially those that centered on personal accountability and being on time. There would be zero tolerance for lateness, not even one minute or fraction thereof, especially for such excuses as unforeseeable traffic. There was no question that they ran a tight ship. I left feeling as if I needed to salute and put on fatigues, but I remained upbeat and staunchly committed.

Mother Nature had a different plan. She sent a ferocious February blizzard to test my resolve. I had heard about a chance of snow, so I made sure I was ready to go by 5:00 p.m. Friday evening. I looked out of the high-rise apartment building where I lived. At least a couple of inches of snow covered the street and traffic was barely moving. What a nightmare! I remembered how Washingtonians panicked in snowstorms, and attempting to drive with people slamming on their breaks and spinning out of control was like playing bumper cars at the amusement park. Nothing was moving in either direction for at least a half a mile back. I phoned my friend—who was now my sponsor in this program—and explained my predicament. He told me that if I were truly committed to being there, I would be there. I asked if he had heard me. There was a full-blown blizzard out there and nothing was moving! He gave me the same response. I said okay and hung up.

"Committed?" I snarled angrily to myself. "I'll show him who is committed." I grabbed my keys and left.

I started up my car, a Plymouth station wagon from another era, and cleared the windshield with a cardboard box that was buried behind the backseat. Then I proceeded to exit the parking lot with the intention of heading eastbound towards DC. I did not make it past the parking lot exit ramp without my first roadblock. The two lanes of cars heading in the same direction were also stuck, blocking my forward movement. People were abandoning their cars in utter desperation and after about twenty minutes of getting nowhere, I did the same.

I locked up and trudged back to my apartment to call my friend and beg him to be reasonable.

After a deadpan silence, he reiterated, "If you want to be there, you will."

Come on! I resented the implication that if I failed to make the class, it was because I was making a choice to dishonor my commitment. But I said nothing. I stormed back to my car. Nothing had changed. The cars were at a standstill, just as they had been when I left to make the phone call. I knew I should have stayed put in the first place and now I had no choice but to stay by my car if I wanted to get it back to a parking place. Nobody was moving and everybody seemed to be waiting for something miraculous to happen that would send us on our merry way.

Three men were walking past me towards the top of the hill. I stopped them and pleaded with them, saying that the only way out of this mess was to start pushing cars. I knew that quite a few of them would have to be pushed before I could even get to mine. This whole situation was unadulterated craziness—almost as fanatical as the internal voice that kept saying, *I will not fail!* They hesitantly obliged and we moved over a dozen cars before we got to my car.

I was elated and thanked them for their help. I climbed back into my station wagon, frozen to the bone and said to myself, "Nothing is going to stop me now." I inched my way over to the far left side of the two-lane highway. My tires spun out again and, no big surprise, I was stuck once more. I was at the forefront of this standstill and there were miles of traffic backed up behind me.

No way! I put my back against the left rear side of the car, grabbed the wheel fender, and with a rush of adrenaline, I pushed the car to slide a few feet toward the exit ramp on the right side of the road. Then I moved to the left front side of the car and proceeded to push the car the same way, zigzagging the whole vehicle across two lanes and into the exit ramp. At last, I was free once again. A woman who was sitting in the car right behind me was watching the whole episode with an incredulous and frightened look on her face. She must have thought I was a prison escapee on the run.

The snow was coming down hard and the roads were already ice-skating rinks. I finally arrived at my destination two hours after I first ventured out my door. The course had started on time at 7:30 p.m. sharp with less than half of the class in attendance. I arrived exhausted but elated at 7:39 p.m. I broke the time commitment, but I had made it. I had defied the odds. I had learned about not accepting defeat. I had learned that there were no limits other than those I imposed on myself. "If you want to be there, you will." How I hated hearing that. Yet it had taken a person of courage to hold truth in front of me. I had stared humiliation in the face and said, "No more!"

I stood before my peers in a breakthrough moment and shared my story. I had closed the door on ever allowing hurt to reach my heart. I listed all the things I felt kept me from being like everybody else, when in truth, they were all the things that kept me from being me.

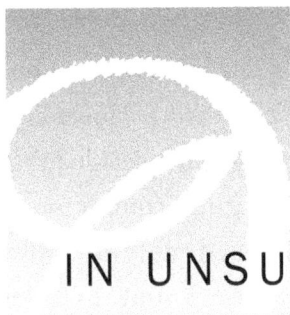

IN UNSUSPECTED PLACES

I accepted a position at Kay Jewelers to tide me over until I could start up a personal training business. Selling jewelry was the last thing I had ever considered, but at least I now had a plan. If the job I wanted did not exist, I would create it myself.

I became great friends with Lazlo, the store manager. He was a Hungarian immigrant and was probably the most generous person I had ever met. He had a room in his house he rented to me. I loved to hear him share the difficulties he encountered in life because he faced them with such gusto for life.

Lazlo helped me to see that the "conditions" in our lives are not real unless we give them permission to stop us. We write our own stories of doom when some condition makes us think that there is no other way—just as I had when I thought that the snowstorm would stop me from attending the seminar. It had not occurred to me *not* to blame the snowstorm and adverse road conditions. After all, I had not created them. I had even congratulated my own good sense when I decided not to drive under those hazardous conditions.

I had asked strangers to help me and had physically pushed cars out of the way so I could pat myself on the back for trying. However, I was still stuck in a story of doom until the moment I decided that nothing was going to stop me from honoring my commitment. In that moment, the story shifted. When I used my own body's adrenaline and heaved my car forward one side at a time, I was set free. The old story reigned only as long as I let it. When I let go of the belief that had stopped me, everything else fell away.

Lazlo had a slight accent but always spoke with passion. "You do not have to understand or know where or how your success will arise, but you need to be very certain that it will." I did not forget that. Most of life's wonderment and conditions are found in unsuspected places.

Had I not worked at Kay Jewelers, I might never have met Rachel, who managed a woman's clothing department at the same mall. These two people unrelated and out of nowhere, did so much to bring joy and balance to my life. Although I was not looking for a serious relationship, there she was, beautiful and caring and falling with me into love as the months passed. I felt my life finally coming together. But just as good things appear, so too, the winds change direction and a different day dawns without the promise of the last.

I never sensed the swell of an impending storm when I answered an early phone call from Brian on what appeared to be the start of an ordinary day. His voice sounded unsure, but he said he had just spoken with Dad. He was calling me, too, because Dad had told him that it was important that he talk with us both in person. Dad had asked to meet us midway between DC and Connecticut, at a New Jersey turnpike rest stop, and wanted to see if we could be there at 2:00 p.m. on Wednesday, which was in two days. Brian warned that Dad had sounded somewhat upset, but would not tell him why, just that he needed to talk to us.

"How weird," I remarked. "This cannot be good."

Dad had said that everyone was fine and he would explain other things in person. I could tell that Brain did not want to be interrogated and wanted off the phone. "If you cannot make it for some reason, I need to call him back. Otherwise it is set," he said.

"Do you think Mom knows this?" I asked.

Brian snapped back. "Mike, I know nothing else, so I will pick you up at 10:30 on Wednesday. And don't be trying to snoop around or call Tracy or Mom. Got it?"

"Okay, but let me know if you hear anything else," I replied. "See you then." And with a hasty click, he hung up.

Brian only lived about a half hour away from me in Maryland, so it made sense for us to go together, but the entire thing was making me unsettled. *What was that all about?* My brain began to reel, wondering what could possibly be so important that Dad would ask for this meeting. I finally had enough of my own relentless speculation and gave up. I did not even tell Rachel or Lazlo.

That Wednesday, Brian and I were silent on the trip up. I tried to sleep, even if just meant closing my eyes to block out the boredom of a straight shot up 95 North to the New Jersey Turnpike. It was clear that Brian did not want to talk about it or hear any of my theories. We made excellent time and arrived about twenty minutes early to the exit. Brian said he was tired and refused to get out of the car, so I just walked around for a while, sensing that he wanted to be alone. I spotted Dad pulling up not far from where we parked. I waved him down, happy to see that he looked fine—physically, at least—and we hugged.

Brian noticed us right away but did not make eye contact. He got out of the car and slammed the door shut with a look of disdain and a faint wave of acknowledgement. He joined us while maintaining a comfortable distance, deliberately lagging a few steps behind. Dad offered to buy us lunch, but within those few minutes the tension had become too thick to consider food. This was going to be a difficult conversation. I had already intuited that much.

Dad had summoned us to this meeting to tell us that he had asked Mom for a divorce. They had separated, as the law required, and he hoped to reach a fair and amicable agreement as soon as possible. The only thing that made sense about the whole meeting was that the New Jersey Turnpike was a fitting place to drop a bomb. The fallout was numbing me to the bone and everything else he said was lost to me. I did not fall apart. I wore the same mask in the door that I wore out. Nothing had been explained. I knew what, but I would never really know why.

In that moment, I became like the rest of the Gannon family. I could turn away, wear the face of a wooden soldier, and march away. Tomorrow would be just another day. There was one thing left to do. I had to call Mom when I got home. She shed a few tears and I unconsciously detached. Before the following year was out, as had been promised, Mr. and Mrs. Gannon were no more. As if the mere act of saying it made it so, I let it go—at least superficially—and retreated to my internal cave. Another storm was looming on the horizon, but I could not predict its arrival.

We naively believe that divorce is an ending that dissolves a marriage between two people. I certainly believed that. The truth is that it is one ending after another. It is the "condition" that silently destroys us, as Lazlo so often cautioned. It is a decree that changes the future history and dynamics of the entire family. It is the ending of family holidays, vacations together, and participation at graduations, weddings, births and deaths. It is the beginning of stepmothers with blended families that remind us of what it was once like to be a family.

We all knew that Mom had been left for another woman. Dad remarried not knowing that one day he would be left to pick up the pieces of his own life. As for me, my own detachment did not alleviate my suffering, as I so arrogantly believed it would. My detachment placed it on hold, but did not subrogate it. There is no grief that lives within us for which we do not eventually pay a price. If we do not recognize and experience pain, then let it go, we compromise our internal landscape and joy will not take root there.

കാങ്കാങ്കാങ്കാ

On a brutally hot and humid late August afternoon, I was more than happy to spend my day off from work inside the air-conditioned house. I was really good about calling Mom, even though the phone was still my nemesis. Since the separation, Mom conveyed an undercurrent of exhausted irritability but always shrouded her feelings with a nauseatingly cheerful voice. I wanted to trust everything was going to be fine, but who really knew? We had all been programmed to display the Gannon smiley face—and voice—to disguise what was inside. Mom was an exceptionally bright woman and I never worried about her ability to take care of herself financially. She already had done well, career wise, in the real estate market, and she carried a serene persona of knowledge and practicality. She was also able to keep the family house in Connecticut in the divorce settlement and had declared that her good friends would always make Westport home. But she vacillated between a place of guarded control and a place of outrage. She was barely contained, like a boiler hovering near its limits.

It took several rings before she picked up the phone and just when I was putting down the receiver, I heard, "Hello," drawn out into labored syllables of slur and confusion.

"What's up, Mom?"

"Oh, hi Mike," she said in a very flat, almost despondent tone, which I ignored.

Our conversation progressed, only because I was doing most of the talking, babbling on about my job, my relationship with Rachel, the hot weather, and anything else to avoid talking about Dad. I could always tell when something had stirred her up. But this time was different. Her answers were strangely distant and her voice left me uneasy. As I spoke, I continued to feel that something was very wrong.

"Mom," I said, "are you okay?"

"Yes, Mike," she replied, and offered nothing more.

"Mom, what's wrong?" I pressed on as only I could do.

There was some hesitancy before she spoke.

"Oh honey, I'm just tired."

"No you're not," I replied. I had begun to realize that she sounded almost woozy. Then, with nothing more than a pure gut feeling, I said, "Mom, you're not thinking about pulling the plug are you?"

"What?" she asked, as if she had not understood what I meant.

"You know, end your life." There, I had said it.

"Answer me Mom!" I demanded. Nothing. Silence.

"Mom, have you taken any pills?"

"Just a few," she said, "but I have a whole bottle right next to my bed."

"And why would that be?" I asked. I could tell she was crying by this time. "Jeez, Mom. Tell me the truth right now. Are you thinking about ending your life?"

Again, no answer.

"Mom, that's it. I'm coming home. Please promise me you won't harm yourself."

"Okay Mike, Okay. I would like for you to come."

"Mom, promise me you will not do anything stupid. Everything is going to be all right." My heart began to race when she failed to answer. I could not even think straight at this point. "Mom I'm going to call 911!"

That got her attention.

"Please, no. Please, Mike," she pleaded. "I'm just fine. Just come home."

Like I could just walk across the street in the next ten minutes. I knew I would make it worse if I threatened to call one of her friends. Tracy was away at college, so I knew she would be alone. I begged her and she gave me her word that she would not take any more pills.

I called Rachel immediately, desperate to hear a comforting voice and have reassurance that Mom would be okay. We talked for about an hour. I explained that I had no choice but to go and I could not promise when I would be back. I was freaking out about Mom and, to my surprise, Rachel was freaking out about our relationship. The thought of losing my mother was racing through my mind, and the more she spoke about how I needed to think this through, the more convinced I became that my decision was the only one I could live with. Going home was not going to be a weekend stay; I needed to be with her until I felt certain she would be okay, however long it took.

I packed my car the night before I left so I could get an early morning start. I fell into bed exhausted, but too upset to sleep. I had never realized until that moment how much Mom meant to me. I felt her love and how often her determination had given me strength. I felt as if I were going through a dark and unfamiliar tunnel, in which my mother's voice echoed a quiet desperation.

I must have drifted off to sleep and into a dream state. I was standing over Mattie's coffin, noticing the stillness of his fragile frame. Instead of looking down at Mattie, I was seeing Mom in his tiny coffin. She appeared so small and frail. I screamed as loud as I could but there was no sound coming from my voice. I awoke in a pool of sweat and jumped into the shower. I had to leave immediately. *Please, dear God, let her be okay.*

I left Virginia and headed north well before the sun came up. I passed the exit on the New Jersey Turnpike where Dad had met Brian and me. I wondered how he had told Mom. I had never asked. How weird to think of our father with another woman, knowing our mother had sacrificed so much to raise her family. It made me queasy to think about it, so I blocked it out and concentrated on driving as fast as possible. Traffic was starting to build up the closer I got to the New York City exits. I barely crawled through the rush hour, ready to explode from the tension in my body. I grabbed the wheel and screamed an expletive just to release the pressure in my chest.

I had called Lazlo before going to bed and he had totally understood. He encouraged me to take whatever time I needed. He knew the deep connection of family all too well.

"Mike, no questions asked, you must go."

He was such a once in a lifetime type of friend. I could always count on him. I knew this would put him in a bind at work, but he refused to accept any apology. He kept repeating, "Just go. Don't think, just go."

I wished Rachel had been as understanding. I knew she was just scared and reacting to the abruptness of my leaving, but once I got a better handle on things, it would be okay. The traffic abated, at least a bit, and I pressed on, driven by one purpose, exceeding the speed limit to make up time. I needed to walk through that door and see for myself that my mother still had the whole bottle of pills next to her dresser—and not in her gullet.

After what seemed like hours since we had spoken over the telephone, I saw her face and I took her in my arms. We both cried. In the days and weeks that followed, I would come to know my mother in new ways. Her pain was raw and uncensored. Even the very thought that she needed to "let go" fiercely stabbed her pride. Sometimes it took constructive baiting on my part to give her anger a voice that was not about blame. I felt her unprocessed indignation erupt and pass through her like a transient madness that had been bottled up inside for most of her life. Her rage erupted like hot blood foaming from her lips and she refused to seek professional counseling.

It hurt to see her like this and I realized even though it had almost been a year since the divorce, she needed to move from the edge at her own pace. I promised myself to hold her heart and stay until I was sure she was in a much better place emotionally.

The more I explained this to Rachel, the harder she tugged at me for reassurance I could not give her. She exposed a side of herself that I had not experienced, a side that felt self-absorbed and shallow. It upset me when she insisted that I didn't care how she felt and that I was overreacting to my mother's mental state. What did she really know about Mom? My daily telephone conversations with Rachel wore me down. I always felt the need to defend myself and the calls usually ended in misunderstanding. I would tell her that the last several months with her had been the best of my life and this situation was only a bump in the road, but it did not seem to matter. I invited her to come for a weekend and go to New York City, but when she did come, the dynamics between us were push-pull. I could not convince her that being with Mom was something I needed to do and that it had nothing to do with us.

Rachel decided that we would have to call it quits if I could not tell her when I would be back. After my second month away she gave me the ultimatum. I told her I respected her decision but it did not change anything for me. She believed Mom should be well enough by then to take care of herself and I was just using her problems to avoid my own life. She may have been right, but I was not taking that chance.

Tracy left college after one year and, as an addendum to her parental divorce trauma, became involved with abusive men. She stuffed her pain by eating and drinking beer and ballooned to well over two hundred pounds. She and Mom bickered incessantly.

Brian remained totally self-absorbed and totally disconnected from Dad. There was no way he would rally around the family, but we never spoke of it to each other. Doug visited both Mom and Dad, but he was very difficult to manage and Mom did not need any more stress at this time in her life.

It opened my eyes to how easily we are able to turn our backs on others. For as long as I could remember, my family had bought into the story of how strong we all were—while watching each other's lives crumble. The unspoken rules of the game were simple: Act like you don't see it, don't take a chance on the real truth, and, at all cost, don't speak up. What would the neighbors say if we violated the family rules and let the world see us as we really were? They might talk about us. Of course, they were doing that anyway. Still, we told ourselves that it was no one else's business. That allowed us to hold on to our precious pride, even though the price tag was exorbitant.

What about accepting the reality that life can be messy no matter who you are? You get your hands dirty and your heart broken, you get shit thrown in your face, but at least you *feel!* You are alive and you are living in your truth because it belongs to you no matter how gritty it gets. Why sell your heart into the slavery of living the "the perfect life" when everyone you are trying to impress already knows it is a lie? You are the only one convinced otherwise. What happens when this false identity, so overflowing with protection, becomes incontinent and spills over into the plastic-lined adult underwear that keeps you safe? You continue the deception and choose to wear the toxic, urine soaked underwear, praying that no one smells the stench. The ego knows no shame and, as a family, we had perfected the art of leading with our egos. But I was beginning to feel uncomfortable with it.

While I could have left when the dust started to settle with Mom, staying seemed much kinder. I stayed. I accepted a job at a small local health club and renewed my passion to one day have my own personal training business. As winter finally retreated into silent hibernation and yellow daffodils colored the Connecticut landscape, my dreams began to take on new life as well. I would lie awake at night and envision the many clients that needed my services. I would go over their diets and formulate tailored exercise programs for each of them. I would practice what it felt like to train these individuals and see them reach their goals.

In what seemed like vision manifesting as life, a physician friend called me and asked if I would be interested in starting up and running a medical weight loss program as a subsidiary to his practice. He wanted me to run my own program and offer nutritional counseling and an exercise program for individuals who were morbidly obese. I accepted immediately. I had only one reservation when I toured the clinic and was introduced to the staff on my first day. His receptionist was very seriously overweight and she would be the person greeting the clientele. She had become an integral part of his practice and I felt it would have been in poor taste to flag the obvious, shall we say, "elephant in the living room." However, I did not want to overlook the message it gave to our clients and, after a few weeks, offered to include her in the program. She was not receptive and I learned my first lesson in tact and employment discrimination. The subject of her weight was taboo.

Despite the rough beginning she was truly a very capable and devoted employee, as well as a locally acclaimed psychic.

IN UNSUSPECTED PLACES

Business was slow in the beginning, so she would tell me about her insights from what she referred to as "the other side." She was highly intuitive and could immediately sense which clients would be successful with the program and what they needed in the way of encouragement. I had an insatiable quest for self-improvement and her talent fascinated me. I was a willing student when she offered to teach me how to tap into my highest good.

Money and sex were always her favorite topics and she could expound prolifically about either. But when I overheard one of the women in the office call her Triple X, I naively thought it related to her dress size rather than being a pornographic reference. Perhaps it was part of my "I will not hear you" syndrome, but I did not recognize it when she started to exceed the boundaries of friendship. Beneath her interest in my success, she wanted the other "S" word and, in particular, she wanted it from me. When I did realize that this was her intent, I didn't quite know what to do. If there was a socially acceptable way to say that I was not attracted to her, no one had filled me in on the protocol. I did enjoy her friendship and was truly grateful for the support she gave me in my work, it was a definite "no go" beyond that.

Within two weeks or so of my realization, divine intervention gave me the perfect exit strategy. While the overall weight loss program was successful, the center as a whole had not yet turned a profit. The physician had done no marketing of the program and I felt it was not going to get off the ground unless he did. I had been away from Virginia for over a year and the time had come for me to think about reestablishing my personal and professional life there.

Thankfully, Mom was past the danger zone and making steady improvements towards acceptance and establishing her own life. One evening at dinner, I felt it was time.

"Mom, are you going to be all right?"

She knew immediately what I meant, that I wanted to return to Virginia.

"Yes, Mike, I absolutely think that now I will be fine."

"Okay, then," I said. I knew we did not need to have any further discussion. "I will call to make arrangements with friends in northern Virginia who may be willing to take me in temporarily. I am ready to go home and start my own business."

There, I had said it. I was going home, and Virginia was my home. My eyes welled up with tears. "Mom, you know you mean the world to me."

She conjured up a soft smile and said, "I know honey, and I really do appreciate you being here with me during these times. Now go do what your heart tells you and remember how much I will always love you."

She gave me her blessing with a hug. And suddenly, as if the sun had burned through an impenetrable bank of clouds, everything seemed to light up. The divorce had not robbed us of our souls. There was life within and around us.

We had faced pain together and learned from each other. She had persevered and had given me the strength to persevere against all odds and to follow my own dream.

"Never, ever give up. Look for life to emerge in the most unsuspected places," she said.

It already had.

SINCE YOU WENT AWAY

The state of Virginia, considered the gateway to the South, is located midway between New York and Florida. Historically referred to as the "birthplace of the nation," it is endowed with a rich heritage dating back to the first Jamestown settlement in 1602. Geographically, it is nestled in the Appalachian, Shenandoah, Allegheny, and Blue Ridge Mountains and outlined by unspoiled jagged beaches that trace miles of the Atlantic coastline.

Driving home from Connecticut I realized I would probably return to see Mom or celebrate the holidays but other than that, my northern roots had finally been severed. Leaving this time meant flying solo. I gave myself a well deserved thumbs-up as I drove past the oversized road sign that read "Virginia Welcomes You," painted with its familiar state bird, the cardinal. I recalled that the cardinal is one of the species that does not migrate. He remains through the hardship of each winter and his bright red plumage can be easily seen speckling the backdrop of a snowy day. Maybe it was a sign that I, too, was here to stay. With only an hour left to go, the state song, whose lyrics read, "Carry me back to Old Virginia," precisely represented my state of mind.

I had stayed in touch with my friend and sponsor from the personal development class and contacted him as soon as I decided to leave Westport. It turned out to be sheer coincidence that he had just decided to rent one of the rooms in his townhouse and he lived precisely in the location where I had planned to work.

Another group of young entrepreneurs on the cutting edge of personal training opened a studio and were looking for a trainer with more expertise and experience than a remedial certification. My credentials far surpassed those of the younger trainers starting to flood the market, so I also landed immediate employment. The only drawback was that I needed to establish my own clientele before I could earn enough money to survive. However, I was convinced a part-time weekend bartending position could supplement my earnings.

Everything seemed to show up in perfect sync, but I still had not connected the dots. The time I spent engaged in the imagery of having the perfect job and place to live had coincided with their materialization in my life. I just enjoyed the creativity of allowing my thoughts and emotions to take me to where I was happiest and most content. What I needed most was a break from the intensity of paying attention in order to hear and from the stress of trying to decipher words and meaning. Instead of turning to a television program with barely audible conversation, I created my own scenarios in my mind. Picturing myself living in a nice house surrounded by friends and seeing myself in the ideal job generated the type of feeling I loved.

I was totally unaware that this process of going within was moving my life in the direction of my choice. I was unaware of something called the law of attraction and that my thoughts and feelings created my reality. Aware or not, it was working in my life. I could see and feel and unknowingly act as if it was already really there, for pure entertainment value. I submitted an unintentional requisition for what I wanted in life by acting it out in my mind, totally without attachment to outcome.

A few days after I had settled in, Jake and I were sitting in the family room drinking a beer. The phone rang—which, of course, I did not hear—and Jake handed it to me saying, "It's for you." Who could have possibly tracked me down? I had not even given Mom my new number yet.

"Hello, this is Mike," I announced.

The voice on the other end of the line sounded low and raspy.

"Well, of course I know it is you, Mike."

"Excuse me," I said.

"I don't think so," she scoffed, like some vixen out of a low budget movie. "What makes you think you can just sneak out of town?"

Oh my god, it was Triple X!

"Oh, hi Lucy," I said, managing to draw out the syllables with forced enthusiasm. "I was thinking about you on my way back to Virginia."

"Oh really? How so?" she cooed.

I clearly did not mean it in the context she insinuated, so I just ignored it and kept right on talking.

"I forgot to get copies of the promotional packets we handed out to clients that included diet and workout regimes and I remembered you had taken a stack home with you."

"What are they worth to you, doll?"

Did she say, "doll?" She had to be drinking because that was when she acted the most annoyingly provocative.

"How did you get my number?" I asked, just to change the subject.

"I am mortified to say I had to ask your mother. She knew the friend's name you are staying with, so I called directory assistance."

We talked for a few minutes and I lightened up somewhat, knowing we were 350 miles apart.

"I'm sorry. I didn't mean to leave without saying good-bye, but things went down so fast."

"I like that," she chortled.

And again I totally ignored the sexual implication. I had already reached full throttle on the repulse meter. I managed to end the conversation with the usual pleasantries about keeping in touch. It was the wrong thing to say.

"Oh, I would like that," she squealed.

It was hard enough to keep the English language straight when you did not hear, but double entendres always "screwed" me up. Lucy did not take the hint when I became increasingly less available, but she did send me the brochures and eased up on the provocative banter. She could be an interesting conversationalist, an amazing business resource, and I had to admit, a loyal friend. Her insights triggered my voracious appetite to learn more about what she called "consciousness" and "inner knowing." She was a remarkable teacher, but I did not want to take advantage of her gifts at the expense of fueling any pretense of a relationship. I understood that men and women relate differently to opposite sex friendships and walk a slippery slope if one or the other decides to change the rules or withholds an unspoken expectation. I was hesitant to rerun the "friendship" speech because I knew she would spin her typical premise that all men secretly wanted her. I felt as if I teetered on the brink of an unbalanced seesaw and if I jumped off first, I would send her plummeting through the earth.

A few months after I moved I received an alarming message on our house answering machine.

"Don't be surprised if you find me one day on your doorstep."

Okay, that was not happening! Mistake number one, I had not addressed it openly from the onset. At the very least, I should have closed the door on her sexual innuendos once and for all. She certainly had been very straightforward with me about not participating in the obesity clinic and that it was offensive for me to ask. So why did I need to worry so much about upsetting her when *she* was offensive? Mistake number two, I felt as if ignoring the remarks allowed me to take the high road, but unfortunately this tactic never knocked her off course. Mistake number three, I shared this dilemma with my older brother Brian. He clued me in on his hypothesis that all women like to be treated like shit and that if I tried to immobilize her sexual advances she might take it as a real come-on. I chalked it up to his perverse sense of humor, but could not rule out, with any certainty, that he had meant it—or that he was wrong. I also considered telling her I was dating someone seriously, but knowing she was psychic, I feared she would sense my dishonesty. Mistake number four, and by far the granddaddy of them all, I did nothing. I reached the frazzled conclusion that I had never agreed to anything and had never given her any reason to believe we were anything other than friends—and if she showed up on my doorstep, I could certainly outrun her.

I loved my job and enjoyed working one-on-one with clients, training them, and implementing diet programs. It did not take long to develop my own following, but we were rapidly outgrowing the space and practically stepping on one another. Fortunately, I had not signed a noncompete clause and had no other financial investment in the business, so I could conceivably train my clientele in another facility. Around the time I had made my decision to move, they did the same, which freed me of any guilt in steering my clients elsewhere.

I incorporated and launched my own independent personal training company at one of the nearby leading sporting clubs of northern Virginia. Most of my clients followed me and I was able to keep a much higher percentage of my income and direct the program. I loved the independence of creating my own schedule in a state-of-the-art facility with many more amenities and prospects for a social life. Within a few weeks, I met Caroline at the health food bar and dared myself to ask if I could join her for lunch. She matched my boldness and replied, "I was just about to ask you the same." Within less than a month we were inseparable.

Caroline could be described as distinctively attractive with blonde hair, a very finely chiseled face, and a sparkling smile. But I could never understand why her eyes wandered in sadness. She could be sullen and pensive in one moment and be charged with enthusiasm and spirit in the next. It felt so satisfying to be in a relationship again with so many unexplored dimensions. I learned the language of introspection with her and each moment felt intense.

She was naturally outspoken in many ways, which balanced my shyness. I loved her outrageous spontaneity, even when it bolted me off my feet the night she asked at dinner, "Are we getting married?"

I wanted to explode with joy but the pragmatic part of me held back, not wanting to fall hopelessly over the edge. I responded with a reassuring smile, rather than the rapture that consumed my heart, "One day. I certainly hope so."

I summoned the courage to tell Lucy about Caroline, hoping she would finally relinquish any relationship notions. When I told her, I could sense the disappointment and her forced façade of being happy for me. She remained silent for a few weeks and then blurted out, "I'm surprised you have not asked me if I have any insights about Caroline." Before I had a chance to respond she continued, "Mike, please listen to me. I feel I need to tell you to go very slowly with her. She has insecurities that will end up hurting you. You are totally blindsided by her cunning ways."

Somewhat shocked but mostly hurt, I thanked her for her concern and disregarded her insights as a manipulative move. About a week later I found a note on the windshield of my car from Caroline. She wrote only a few sentences saying that she could no longer see me and that she hoped that I would forgive her. Her explanation was that her life had been spinning out of control and it would be best for her to figure things out alone. None of this made any sense to me. My eyes darted around the parking lot looking to see if she was nearby waiting for my reaction or to talk. I was consumed with finding her and immediately drove to her house and rang her doorbell. Her face froze as she opened the door.

"Can I come in please?" I asked in an almost pleading tone, trying hard to appear rational rather than totally crushed.

"Sure," she replied. We sat and we briefly talked, but she made it clear there would be no going back for her. She was scared and confused about how she was feeling and wanted to protect herself from getting hurt before it was too late.

"Too late for what?" I kept asking.

"I don't know. I'm having strong feelings and I want to make sure I know what I am getting into."

"Well, you will never know if you leave," I replied.

She was intent on being alone to figure it out. I was devastated at the thought of being without her, and I could never have come from a place of pride where I pretended otherwise. I felt this was not a time-out, it was good-bye, so I turned away to put on my jacket and wipe the tears from my eyes. I gently moved her face towards mine to speak the only truth I knew.

"Good-bye, Caroline. You have no idea how you broke my heart."

And I left.

"Why, God," I muttered to myself. "What else do I need to do?" I understood that asking a rhetorical question meant you should not expect an answer, but I did. For the next two weeks, night after night, I lay in bed with a tender heart, waiting by my phone for the magical call that she had changed her mind. Why is it that we wait for another to stop our suffering when we inherently know we are in charge of healing our own pain? Yet the roller-coaster ride through the highs and lows of vulnerability refused to stop.

We had talked about having children and maybe that was her concern. My family did have an unfortunate track record with genes. Not once had she voiced a concern or any other hesitancy about us as a couple, leaving me totally baffled. Finally, I put an end to my runaway emotion. *Enough!* I had to let go and accept that the relationship was over. I had to reopen my heart and invite love in without bitterness and attachment to the past.

I did not tell Lucy that we had broken up and yet, on the very same day that I reached this conscious decision, she called.

"Mike, I am sorry things didn't work out for you."

I almost dropped the phone. How did she know? It was really beginning to upset me, so I asked her.

She said, "The best way for me to tell you is to teach you how to have these types of insights yourself. Mike, you can come to understand these things long before they hurt you, but first you need to clear your thoughts of Caroline from your energy field. Can you do that?" she asked.

"I have already," I offered in response.

"Good, that is where we will start."

I had not remembered agreeing to anything, but if she could teach me, I was open to learn anything that would stop the pain. I had a new respect for Lucy and I was thankful I had not let our friendship lapse. I could deal with her idiosyncrasies if she could teach me these valuable skills. She had always assured me it was not a gift, but an art that needed constant practice and refinement.

I began to picture the woman I wanted to spend my life with. I did not need the addiction I had experienced with Caroline, but I craved the spiritual component that transcended everyday thinking and beliefs. I connected with what I had called my God space—my wordless, soundless connection to the divine. I could feel the emotional poison of jealousy, comparison, and judgment in others and myself and knew this drove relationships to the brink of personal hell. I tried to keep my thoughts away from what I didn't want because I had figured out, on some level, that what I didn't want would be what I would get if I thought about it too much. I needed softness and compassion, but I also needed strength and commitment.

Interesting that these were all the things I also needed to work on in myself. How could I ask of another what I did not yet have to give? I had opened another door for my own self-improvement and, strangely enough, that always made me happy. I found that people liked to think of themselves as just fine the way they were, but I never envied that trait. Some called it being self-confident, but I often felt it was the mask of fear. I wanted my fear out of me, not *in* me, and I was just about to enter a stage in my life that would teach me why.

It seems that the universe, in its ultimate wisdom, always throws out the test first and the lesson afterwards. We accept the belief that we go to school, learn the lesson, and then take the test. If becoming an "A" student were all there was to life, it might work. But we learn what we need after we jump off the cliff with most tests.

Could it have been beginner's luck when Brittany walked through the front door of my life with a bright and shining hello? Born and raised in England, everyone nicknamed her "Brit." Her accent and contagious laugh sparked attention the moment she entered a room. I played it differently and did not immediately ask her out, even though I knew she was interested. This time I would forego a race to the finish line. It felt good just to be back in the game. I looked forward to seeing her when she came in to work out and, fortuitously, she finished up about the same time that I had a break in my schedule. I relished every moment of getting to know her. I was never quite sure when it would be safe for me to open my heart, but I also needed to throw away the book of 101 excuses for being absent.

I went home to Connecticut for Thanksgiving feeling resurrected from heartbreak. Mom was in a much better place and happy to have her brood with her for the holiday. It was strange to think that Dad was now remarried and with a whole new family, but I had learned that painful endings were part of life's march through evolution. My anticipation of a new relationship with Brit had softened the harsh reality of severed ties and I was back on the road to Virginia after a few days with family.

I was grateful to be able to unplug from the noise of traffic and the excitement of the holidays. I placed my hearing aid next to me on the passenger seat and drove undisturbed in that place of inner connection. I wondered if I just did this because of my ability to disconnect from all sound or if hearing people went to this same space. It allowed me to listen from within. Was it God, or my higher self, or a kinesthetic destination? I never felt the inclination to give it an identity. It begged the question, how does connection originate? I felt energetic connection before I had words to describe it. The word did not make it real, the feeling did. It was not something you could talk about with just anyone. I would have conversations with my clients about things—new cars, good restaurants, nice houses, the economy—but never much about well-being outside of the fitness arena. I missed those types of conversations with Caroline.

I could not always be certain if hearing people experienced their inner world as much as I did. I spent so much time in silence that my inner world was as rich and important to me as my outer world. Did no one ever talk about this?

Was it my disability that allowed me to soar in worlds of silent understanding or was this type of introspection only the musing of child's play I had never left behind?

I was haunted with the possibility that my emotional processes were different than those of others in many ways. Language is known to transform experience and my linguistic adeptness was compromised during my early years. Being in the early developmental stages without much auditory function, my world had depended on visual and kinesthetic perception. I processed some thought without verbal symbolic representation. I was delayed in moving from a world of images to the specificity of concepts once words were introduced. My early emotional development had not had a vocabulary that defined how I felt, but that did not mean that I did not experience the inner state. The early studies involving profoundly deaf people warned of a thwarted ability to emotionally relate to others. Yet I often wondered if hearing people knew about the white light that lifts your spirit within without words. If they did, no one ever talked about it. If I was feeling afraid, when my hearing aids were off I could see a white light around me and I would feel protected. The need for answers spun around inside me like the balls inside the lotto machine. I wanted to reach in and extract the winning answer.

I arrived back to work to hear the complaints of clients with overstuffed bodies from the holiday feeding frenzy. There could be no mercy when excess calories pleaded to be burned. At around 6:00 p.m., just before my last client, Brit breezed through the door with a brown bag in her hand and a warm, "Hi there!" She handed the package to me.

"It's from England. I thought you might like it," she said, and walked off to the locker room. I was dumbfounded and speechless. It was a six-pack of Watkins beer and more than an unexpected surprise, it was my "in" to ask her out. I trained my last client hoping she did not leave before I finished. In almost perfect synchronicity, as my client said good night, Brit emerged from the locker room, ready to go. We sat down for about an hour at the fruit bar and ended the evening with a date planned for that Friday night. I went home feeling hesitantly amazed at what was unfolding. *Give it time*, I thought to myself.

Friday night finally arrived and I met Brit at the gym so we could head into DC to see the production *Defending the Caveman*. As I waited for her with butterflies assaulting my stomach, I noticed Caroline at the juice bar with her work crowd. I knew she would see me leave with Brit because she seemed to be keeping her eye on me. She had, no doubt, noticed that I was all dressed up. Brit walked through the door looking absolutely stunning. We greeted each other with radiant smiles and left hand in hand. I could see through the reflection in the glass door that Caroline could not take her eyes off us.

We arrived at the theater at L'Enfant plaza, amidst a cold drizzling rain, but it did not dampen the mood. Once the performance was under way, the raucous laughter was contagious, even though I missed most of the fast paced monologue. Dinner gave us an opportunity to connect. I felt relaxed and any thoughts of Caroline were a distant haze.

The month of December was a whirlwind of excitement between us and I was no longer reminding myself to proceed with caution. I knew she would be going back to her family in England to spend Christmas, so we celebrated before she left and promised to ring in the New Year together. I could still smell the delicate floral scent of magnolia from her perfume lingering on my shirt hours after we said good-bye at the international gate very early that morning. Much later that day, I saw a newsbreak flash across the television screen in the gym lobby. Pan Am flight 103 had exploded over Lockerbie.

Oh my god! Brit had left on Pan Am, but I did not know her flight number or how it was routed. I knew that Americans were onboard but had not heard that the flight had originated in Heathrow and was en route to John F. Kennedy airport. This was well before the days of twenty-four-hour news coverage and I was at work, isolated from the news. What if she was on that plane? I felt the rush of "what ifs" shred my heart. I was still training clients late that night at the gym, clamoring for information. When my pager went off, it triggered sheer terror. Who could possibly be paging me? I grabbed the club phone to check in for my messages. Finally, a familiar voice.

"Mike, I just wanted to say hi and I already miss you, Love. Bye!"

Thank god, she was safe. I loved her accent and how she called me "Love." I played that message over and over again in her absence as my confirmation that she was still very much alive.

Christmas in Westport, Connecticut with the family always held certain expectations and provided a traditional form of holiday flair. Mom told Brian to sit in Dad's empty chair for Christmas dinner. He refused. There was comfort in knowing that Mattie's grave was only miles away, but the aftermath of divorce left no such tribute of loving remembrance. I was relieved when Christmas dinner was over.

Just like at Thanksgiving, I knew Brittany was the best reason I had to get back on the road home and into her arms. I waited at Dulles International Airport for all the passengers to trickle through customs before she came through the door. We were like two kids struck with puppy love and full of stories to tell. Happy New Year, 1989!

Within a month's time I was beginning to notice that Caroline was frequenting the gym more often than usual. I wanted to believe it might have been part of a New Year's resolution to work out, but I knew better. Her timing always seemed to coincide with my presence. One particular evening, she was socializing with a group of her friends from work by the fruit bar and they all waved me over to their table. I reluctantly obliged. I sensed her frustration as I spoke to one of the other women first. Before I had a chance to say much at all, she slipped off to the restroom. I was too naive to figure out that her friend was setting me up. She began telling me that the separation between Caroline and me had made Caroline aware of how much she really felt for me and that she did not know how to tell me. I kept thinking, *I don't need to hear this!*

"Mike, you need to understand that she has a hard time expressing her feelings and she would like to get together to talk about it."

"I need to understand?" I retorted. "It's a moot point! We're over!"

Caroline returned before her friend could fully respond and I bolted. I felt that she should have been adult enough to come to me directly if she had something to say, at which point I would have told her myself. She had broken up with a note on my car, so I was not surprised by her indirectness. I deserved better than secondhand information.

I left the gym and my resolve began to weaken as I buckled myself into the driver's seat. The love I'd once had for Caroline began to resurface and gain momentum—along with memories of our amazing sexual chemistry. "Stop it!" I demanded of myself, and I sped off to see Brit.

She was delighted with my surprise visit and the moment she opened that door, I felt a sense of grounding that put a temporary standstill to my spiraling whirlwind of emotions. When I left for work the following morning, she kissed me on the forehead and thanked me for surprising her. I felt instant guilt. I knew the surprise was less a loving gesture on my part than a desire to be rescued from my relapse of emotions towards Caroline.

For days I experienced unwanted backflips, which sent me back to disruptive thoughts of Caroline. Caroline's friend must have relayed our conversation to her because I heard nothing from her. The one thing that kept coming back to me was the explosive sexual chemistry I had felt for her. With Brit I felt a mellower, less intense relationship, but so many other things outweighed the lack of intensity.

Just when I felt out of the woods with the entire drama, I found Caroline waiting for me by the front entrance of the gym and there was no way to avoid her. I resisted any altercation. I knew she would have her word with me and I wanted to put it to rest. I had to respect that she had given me the opportunity to talk when I came to her door despondent the night of our breakup. I could at least set the record straight and tell her, face-to-face, that we were not getting back together. I let her explain that she had only meant for the separation to be a time-out for her to truly identify her feelings. She admitted that during the time apart she had become totally conscious of and overwhelmed by how strongly she felt about us.

I remained silent and listened, but I resented the word "us." There *was* no more "us." No way! What infuriated me and took me totally off guard was that, before I had a chance to respond, she demanded to know about my relationship with Brit. I slammed back at her, "Well if you must know, we are very serious and I have absolutely no intention of resuming a relationship with you."

She immediately burst into tears. I regretted my outburst and recalled being in her shoes, begging for things to be different. I knew that place of denial and hurt, and I had not intentionally meant to throw it back in her face. I put my arms around her to give her a comforting gesture of understanding and said, "I'm so sorry, but it's over between us." I needed to make it final so we both could move on with clear understanding. She cried even harder and embraced me tightly. I could feel her shuddering pain and implicitly knew how immense her rejection felt.

In a split second of confusion over lost love, I felt a surge of feeling for her rush back into my heart and I knew she felt it as well. I panicked, pulled away from her, and left without another word. I had to put her out of my mind. I felt cruel. I had, in my own way, paid her back. But I had done it with the blistering fear of my own resurging emotion. How could loving her less and casting her out of my life bring me closer to Brit? How could I ever think that my love for Brit would flourish at Caroline's expense?

Denial plays wonderful tricks. Within days I had rationalized everything and was actually feeling thankful that this was the way it had to be. Life was good again. Brit and I often compared our relationship to that of two puppies because we loved to nuzzle, wrestle, play, and eat. We thoroughly cherished the simplicity of an uncomplicated relationship. She embraced my deafness, making sure that I was both heard and understood by others. Her patience and total acceptance of me was an extraordinary act of love and I felt blessed beyond belief.

And then came Valentine's Day. Valentine's Day is not always a day to remember your love. It can be a bittersweet day when love is lost. Caroline showed up to remind me. She insisted she needed to say one more thing to me in private and her sense of urgency alarmed me. I feared that there could be a very public scene if I did not comply. She began by accepting full responsibility for the breakup and that she could not live with herself without saying how sorry she was for what she had done. Wasn't this old news? I told her I understood but added that there would be no more conversations.

Predictably, in a week or so she returned with more determination than ever. Brit sensed my mood swings whenever Caroline made contact with me and would ask if everything was all right.

This insanity had to stop. I decided to pay a visit to Caroline at her house. As soon as we sat down to talk, all I could think of was taking off her clothes. I decided to ride it out like a wave as she inched herself closer to me. I managed to hold back until she reached across me and ever so teasingly brushed her hand across my thigh. That was all it took for our rampant sexual energy to consume us both.

I again left her house consumed with guilt and utter shame over what had just transpired. Who had I become? I went straight home to a scalding shower to remove any trace of the musty smell of sex. I felt like a motorcycle at full throttle held stationary, the rubber of my integrity peeling away in the process. How had I gotten myself into this unbelievable predicament? Brit was decidedly the more stable of the two. She was smart, educated, fun loving, and strikingly adorable. Caroline was a Joan of Arc type who would burn at the stake for what she believed in, but she lacked the finesse and softness that so fed my soul. But my self-created drama over choice had little to do with either woman. Why was I allowing myself to cross those boundaries that had once been so clear?

One more time I asked Caroline to honor my wish to be with Brit. She stormed off in a tantrum but we both knew that she would be back to ruffle more feathers. And I was addicted to her return.

Caroline made sure I saw her at the club and let me know she felt Brittany was a mistake I tolerated. One night, late after work, she quietly waited to speak to me in private. When I said, "Absolutely not," she threatened to say what she had to say right then and there. I followed her to safety.

"Mike, I love you so much, and I know what I did hurt you terribly, but I would do anything to be with you again," she said.

I knew this could get worse and with her proclivity for outbursts, I did not want the remaining patrons to hear the altercation. I willingly ushered her to my car, hoping to squelch any scene. She said she did not care how long it took for me to see that we should be together.

"Okay, Caroline. I hear you, but you are only torturing yourself," I replied softly, knowing I was doing the same.

With that, she sat back with her eyes wide and said, "Mike, hurry up and go around the parking lot! Hurry!"

"Why?" I asked.

"Just do it!" she commanded.

I immediately felt someone had seen us, so I drove around the building.

"Pull in right there! And turn off the lights!" she said.

I pulled into the dimly lit parking spot, put the car in park, and before I could say another word, she exited the car. Now I was sure someone was on to us. Otherwise she would not have gotten out. Before I knew what she was doing, she was on my lap facing me while closing the door behind her. I literally could not move.

"What are you doing?" I asked.

"Shhh, kiss me," she whispered.

"I can't," I muttered pathetically.

"Yes you can. Kiss me!" she persisted.

Her lips barely touched mine as she began slowly rotating her hips. "Don't do this," I insisted as she continued to writhe. Then I began to plead, but to no avail.

"I just don't want to go home again with you not knowing for sure that this is it," she said. "Every time we get back together, you feel the same attraction, but it intensifies because you know there is so much more to who we were as a couple. You didn't fall in love with the sex, you fell in love with *me*. You stay with Brit because of how much I hurt you. You feel comfortable and at ease with her, but there is no passion in your life and I know you know that and I know one day you will live to regret what we might have had. You have always wanted to be accepted, to have friends. And now you do and she is one of them. But she will never be your true love. She will never take you to that place where you will grow and be inspired. That is why I was afraid and pulled away. I knew you were different. I knew our connection was spiritual and it transcended every boundary I had ever known. *You* are different, Mike. You are special and you have gifts to give to the world—far more than you will ever know."

"How do you know this?" I asked.

"Because in my soul I feel a fire when I am with you. I ignite a spark that connects you to your divinity and just as it frightened me, it frightens you. So you pull away from me, just like I did from you. Let me ask you one thing. If Brit was out of your life, wouldn't you come to me in a heartbeat, just to find out if what I am saying is real? You are much bigger and much stronger than any pain I caused you. I had to tell you that, Mike, and you had to hear it. And whatever you think of me, I had to share this with you. Please do not settle. It will kill you in the end. That is all I ask."

I knew that she was right. Deep down, I knew that puppy love was transient, but I had wanted it so badly that it hurt to be without it. I had to stop going to my head for answers and then convince myself of what I wanted to believe. What was my heart really telling me? I had to risk finding out and no neon signs or strike-me-dead realizations were going to give me the answer.

I did know one thing; I owed it to Brittany to be truthful about my indecision. I did not want to take advantage of her. How could I? I had been taken advantage of all my life. I knew what it felt like. I did not want that for her. I had to let her go. She deserved total commitment and I did not have it to give. I decided to tell her on Saturday, but the very thought of hurting her was unbearable. I hated that my truth meant her pain.

That Saturday, my heart was pounding as I pulled up to the parking spot in front of her red brick townhouse. It literally felt like somebody was beating on my chest. I slowly walked to the front door and took a deep breath. I pushed the doorbell and she greeted me as usual with a full body hug and the warmth of a brilliant summer sun.

"Hi," I said in a tone more businesslike than affectionate. She instantly sensed my mood.

I asked her to sit down with me and began to tell her about my feelings. I didn't want to bring up the issue of infidelity because I wasn't out to destroy her. I said that I couldn't understand how I could love someone as much as I loved her without being able to match that intensity when we made love. I made no comparisons to my lovemaking with anyone else, I just took responsibility for how I felt. And I felt awful. Tears welled in her eyes and she got up and walked back to the kitchen. I gave her a few moments of space and got up to see if she was okay. She was standing over by the trash tearing up a card. Then she threw it in the trash and fled from the kitchen. I could see by its cover that it was meant for me because it had "Puppy" written on it. I pieced it back together and it read: "Mike, from one puppy to another, I have never been so happy with anyone as I have been with you. I hope to spend the rest of my life with you. I love you. Your puppy, Brit."

Could it get any worse? I felt like a complete cad. "I'm so sorry." I tried to give her a hug, but her arms remained crossed in front of her.

"Just go now," she said.

I left devastated with what I had done and the pain I had caused her. I so wanted to fix it, to call her back and say it had all been a mistake, but I feared that I would inevitably hurt her again. I needed a break from all woman, especially Caroline. There would be no reconciliation with her at the expense of another.

One day a few weeks after our breakup, Brittany proudly came back to the gym. I could tell she was upset when she saw me, but she managed a terse hello. I knew that anything more than that would be impossible for a long time to come. I wanted to talk to her. I wanted to make sure she knew how much I had appreciated her, but I could not reopen the wound. It was too new and raw, but I knew it would heal in time. She would bounce back and we would both be wiser for having loved one another. I knew that.

I also knew that I had to give it another try with Caroline. How else would I ever know if it could work between us? First I needed to get away and think things through. Lucy had called the day before and said there was an opening to sign up for a certification program in hypnotherapy. I had looked into it before as an adjunctive tool for my clients who experienced resistance to weight loss. I knew that hypnotherapy had also proved successful for helping people let go of fear and establish more positive lifetime patterns. I was ready to incorporate something new into my career and more than ready to get away, so I flew to New Hampshire for the training.

Even though Lucy would be among the participants, the class would be rigorous, with little time for socializing one-on-one. Once again, within minutes of seeing her, she gave me her insights on my relationship with Caroline, which she insisted faced another terrible demise. I also noticed that she seemed jealous when I mingled with other female participants or when I pressed her for more concrete information about my relationship. She kept repeating herself, over and over again, saying that I needed to move back to Connecticut because she intuited great things would happen for me there that did not include Caroline. She insisted that I needed to spend more time with her so she could teach me how to be psychic. I eventually stopped her dead in her tracks. I knew I would not be returning to Connecticut and I had no plans to spend more time with her. I shifted the focus back to her.

"So how is your love life these days?"

I really didn't want to know, but it was a good diversion. She informed me that she had learned—very successfully—how to practice black magic. She had caught her boyfriend cheating with another woman and said, with a diabolical laugh, that she had used her powers to ensure that he never loved again. My blood ran cold with anything to do with the occult. I made up my mind to get her out of my life, even as a friend, once the conference was over.

The course itself was tremendous and brought a new understanding to my life. I learned that everyone has "limbic" patterns embedded and deeply ingrained in the reptilian part of the brain that cause us to react to triggers. This is where the ego mind resides and where drama plays out, over and over again. I needed to work on this part of myself. My relationship with myself needed to change. I understood that misery was not a payoff, it was the ego's way of remaining arrogant and holding on to its defenses. I had to rely on myself for answers because there was no fast lane to love and human understanding. I closed the chapter on depending on the wisdom of others; it was time to call upon my own wisdom. The more I focused on what was wrong, the more I created it.

I understood that my future, with or without Caroline, was held in a delicate balance. Soul love does not change with the winds of time, but it only flourishes with strong roots and abundant light. I had the feeling another test was just around the corner.

DRAGON IN THE HOUSE

September had always been a month to begin anew. I equated it with starting a new school calendar and, along with that, a renewed commitment to make it my best year ever.

I had just slipped out of my house to clear my head and was contemplating the notion of September as a time for renewal. The air was crisp and I was excited to integrate my hypnosis training into a holistic approach to wellness.

I knew that many issues outside of a person's body could diminish that person's general health. One of the training presenters had emphasized the point that a healthy body arises from an unfettered mind and that hypnosis starts the process. I needed no convincing. I knew that my natural desire to control things took a toll on my relationships with women. As much as I was drawn to Caroline, I still always looked for a smoking gun. I was sick of all the turmoil and bitterness that I had experienced over the previous year, but stood guilty as charged for my own participation. I wondered if there was compelling information on ego dissolving, or was that a course I needed to write myself? When children act out, they generally get sent to "time out." I willingly sent myself. I did not understand that my fears about making a mistake or picking the wrong woman only perpetuated more of the same behavior. Focusing on my anxiety kept it flooding back onto my life stage. I needed a break from the drama. I had no fantasies that romantic love was the be-all of life. I had unsuccessfully tried to avoid the pitfalls of making former lovers the enemy. It was not that the conditions for happiness were absent from my life. I wasn't navigating the road map and staying on course with any precision.

I struggled with myself and what little peace I could find usually ended when the telephone rang. On this particular September day, Caroline was the disrupter of my tenuous peace.

"Mike!" she said with a curious mixture of mystery and desperation as soon as I picked up the phone.

"Ah, yeah?" I replied hesitantly.

"I need to tell you something!"

"What's up?" I asked as cheerfully as I could muster.

"Do you remember the story you told me about your psychic friend Lucy telling you she had placed a hold on her ex-boyfriend so that it would keep him from meeting or falling in love with anybody else?

"Listen to me carefully, Mike. I know she has done it to you!"

I attempted to stop her right then and there.

"Caroline, don't even go there. She has done no such thing."

She totally ignored me and kept right on talking.

"She wanted you to move back up to Connecticut so she could have you for herself and she did not want me in the picture. You told me yourself how strange she acted at the convention, like you were her boyfriend. You said you showed no interest in her. Wouldn't that give her reason to do this thing to you? She doesn't want you to have feelings for me. I know this sounds bizarre, but stuff like this happens and you should stop being so insistent that it is not happening to us. You're not even listening to me," she fumed.

At least now she had stopped long enough to breathe.

"Caroline," I whispered, trying not to broadcast my dirty laundry throughout the neighborhood.

"I am listening to you, but you know I don't get everything on the telephone, so please just bear with me. The history of our past has been one of constant turmoil. You *do* know that?"

"Was that a statement or a question?" she snipped back at me.

"We need to learn from this and take responsibility for our own behavior rather than attribute it to some crazy psychic attack. I'm not trying to dismiss your apprehension, but we need to move on by not pointing the finger at anyone—especially each other."

She interrupted. "See, you did not hear me! I was not pointing the finger at you!"

"Can I finish?" I said. "In the event that you're right in your assumption, then this hold would be on me, not you. If so, I will deal with it. But for now, no more phone calls. We need to be apart for now. Please honor this if you really want things to work out for us."

"How convenient," she scoffed, now on the verge of tears. "But in case you haven't noticed, I'm part of this 'we' equation. So if you're affected by this beast of a woman, so am I. I have been sick with worry over this and you think it can be randomly dismissed because you say so. Sorry for my intrusion."

She hung up.

One thing most hearing people do not understand is that deaf people do not hear the click of a phone hanging up on them, so they keep right on talking to themselves.

"Caroline, I didn't say we're over. You need to understand this, once and for all. Caroline? Caroline?"

Damn!

She had hung up on me before and she had just done it again. So I, too, slammed down the phone, just out of principle. She was clutching for anything she could find to create more commotion, and now I was angry. I felt such a sense of unrequited outrage, but I had no doubt she would be back for another round.

For the time being, I was intent on clearing my mind and retreating to my God space to clean up unfinished business. I removed my hearing aid and instantly felt the amazing void of no sound, where peace and quiet were usually not violated. It was instant relief to hear nothing. I so needed to be in that silent and sacred space, but this time my own mental chatter was incessant. Exasperated, I gave up and slipped back inside the house to go to bed. Sleep had always been my ultimate escape. This time, I lay awake until dawn.

Caroline had tread into risky territory with her speculation about Lucy. Granted, Lucy did have her own set of problems, but she was also a gifted clairvoyant with an uncanny ability to powerfully focus and channel her energies. I did know that much. One day she had put her finger on my forehead and shot a burst of energy into my head that almost knocked me off my feet. In that regard, she had made a believer out of me. But this "psychic hold" on a former boyfriend, I wasn't buying into it, even if I had to admit that I'd felt the darkness of her words. I also had to acknowledge that her bizarre jealously at the convention had troubled me, as well as her mounting disdain for Caroline. But Caroline's inferences were preposterous.

Then I paused to consider the fact that I had not heard from Lucy at all. In fact, the more I thought about it, this was the strangest piece. Normally she would have been on the phone wanting to know how I was coming along with using the hypnotherapy. What if all the time I had been with Caroline there had been some kind of psychic interference disrupting our relationship? The litany of "what ifs" continued their perilous twists and turns on the roller-coaster ride of infinite possibility and ended up in a place called "nowhere," exactly where they belonged. There was power in suggestibility.

One day short of a week later, Caroline phoned again with more of the same accusations about Lucy. However, this time it was different. I felt the negative energy from Caroline invading my space. I kept the conversation short and was careful to not refute what she said. I just listened and let it go. It had already been a long day. I paid some bills, put out my clothes for the next day, and called it a night.

Right before I climbed into bed, I felt my chest tighten as if I were in a pressure chamber—to the point where I had difficulty breathing. Could I be having a heart attack? I lay down hoping it would subside, but it continued. Somehow it felt that the pressure was being externally applied. I felt I was being invaded.

I sat for a few minutes, wondering if I was having a panic attack. I had seen a girl in college have one and she had literally reacted as if she were going to die until it subsided. That had to be it. After all, I had been under a lot of stress, trying to work long hours and then practicing my self-hypnotherapy at night.

I didn't dare to consider that this dark, prickly force field of energy might have come from some unidentified place in my subconscious. However, the feeling returned the minute I started to think about Caroline. I could hardly believe what was happening. I had to get out of the state I was in so I crawled into bed and, at some point, fell asleep.

I woke up the next morning with a debilitating headache. It felt like somebody had taken an air pump and totally inflated my head while I was asleep. I felt nauseous in the shower and considered that I might be coming down with something. I had no time to be sick, I had an entire day of clients. By the time I got to the gym I was feeling worse and put a cold towel on my forehead for some temporary relief before I greeted my first client.

My first client was Martha and, as always, she was ready to go with her ever-enthusiastic smile. It was so good to see her. She had been a loyal client, following me from one facility to another as I carved out my career path. She always brightened my day and, in turn, I kept her in the best shape of her life. We were a superb team.

"What's with you?" she said, looking at me as if I were some grotesque creature out of a horror movie.

"I'm not feeling that well, Martha," I reluctantly admitted.

"Mike, seriously, I feel nothing but negative energy coming from you!" She had unintentionally confirmed my worst nightmare. "Did you and Caroline have another bad fight?" she asked. She knew the two of us had been going through some rough times.

"Martha, you got a minute? I need to tell you something," I said.

"Sure!" she replied as she took off her weight lifting gloves. "This can wait."

I led her to one of the back offices and closed the door behind us. What was I going to say now that I had her undivided attention? Was I going to tell her that a spiteful psychic had me by the shorthairs?

"Martha!" I whispered with intensity, "something strange is going on and I don't know what it is!"

"I can tell that," she replied.

I told her the entire story about Lucy and her black magic and Caroline's insistence that we were now under a spell. She listened intently. Martha was a wonderful, rare woman who embraced life with great passion and a gentle spirit that softened the way she approached life. In recent years she had lost the love of her life to cancer. She had stayed with him until he died in her arms. She had grown up in South America and I enjoyed hearing her stories and experiences with different spiritual practices. She understood things about energy fields, psychic phenomena, and holistic healing.

"Mike, is there more that you are not saying?"

"I really don't know. I have never experienced anything quite like this before."

"Are you depressed?" she asked.

"I could be," I said, "but it doesn't seem like that."

"Mike are you willing to try to let go of this one thought at a time?"

"More than willing!" I responded.

"First of all, I want you to take some deep cleansing breaths and listen very carefully to me." She looked directly into my eyes as if she could see through me.

"You must promise me that you will give this no power whatsoever."

I started to answer her, but she squelched my reply. She spoke in a very firm voice, yet with a hint of caution.

"Mike, do not ever buy into the ploy of darkness, for any reason. You must believe me and hear what I am saying. Replace all doubt and all fear with light, no matter how badly you feel. Surround yourself with a safety net and cocoon of protective light and remain within in it no matter what. Now, I want you to close your eyes and repeat after me, 'I am safe. I am loved.'"

I could hear her voice in my mind as it trailed off into unspoken knowing and I did what she asked. She made me promise I would call her if I needed to talk, but it could not be about darkness or the story about the psychic. She was definitely on to much more than she was saying, and I thanked her profusely for her help. I needed to talk to Caroline and tell her what had happened to me and let her know that she, too, must stop giving this any power.

I decided to go to her office. I knew she always spent time alone there on Saturdays so she could work without the usual disruptions. It was a more neutral place to meet—unlike a house, with the allure of a nearby bedroom. When I pulled open the front door of her office building, I could see her slumped silhouette in the entranceway to her office. She looked the way I felt.

"Something is wrong, isn't it?" I asked.

She answered in a shaken voice, "Mike, oh my god, I don't know what's happening to me!"

"Are you sick?" I asked, hoping that whatever was happening to her might be attributed to some kind of virus. She did not answer the question, but asked one of her own.

"Mike, what about you? How are you feeling? Tell me now!" she demanded, her voice shrill. "I need to know what is happening!"

Now I was really frightened, despite my efforts to surround myself in the light, which had faded quickly upon seeing her. I knew beyond all doubt that something had also happened to her energy field. It felt every bit as virulent as mine.

"Caroline, calm down," I said gently. "It's going to be okay." I put my arms around her as we walked back to her office. The pressure in my chest was building and I remembered Martha's warning to not buy into anything. But nothing other than full concurrence with Caroline's theory about Lucy was going to fly. At least not right now. I carefully worded what I had to say to validate her feelings, but warned her not to give it any more power by panicking. It was evidently the wrong choice of words and set off more hysterics in her.

"Caroline, please! I know you are upset, but we cannot feed into this. I spoke to Martha about it and she said she felt negative energy coming from me. And I feel it coming from you as well."

"Thanks a lot! Glad you believe her and not me."

"I tried to tell you but you don't listen to me," I said. "I promise we will get to the bottom of this, but for now, please get a hold of yourself. Lucy cannot do anything to us if we don't allow it."

"Oh really?" she said sarcastically. "Well, it isn't as if I relinquished permission to her to do this and here we are, so what do you make of that?"

I could not blame her because as much as I was trying to fix it, or at least cope with it, the truth remained that I had no more of an idea than she did where this would take us.

"Caroline, let me take you home. Let's just get some fresh air and shake off these feelings. I know we can do it. Come on. How about a walk?"

She would not move, but sat transfixed with no expression at all on her face. Now I was really beginning to lose it myself. Finally, she stood up, acting as if it was totally her idea, and we both walked out the door in silence. She got into her car and I got into mine. I could not leave things as they were, so I followed her home against my better judgment.

We just sat in her living room, staring at the walls and saying nothing. It was apparent that she did not want to talk so I told her I was going home and asked her to call me, which I knew was a given.

Once home, I retreated to my bedroom and stared at the vacant walls that could not talk back. At least I was grateful for that.

As much as I hated to admit it, things were beginning to come together. Whatever it turned out to be and whether it had come from Lucy or not, it was neither a virus nor a coincidence; it was a dark, negative energy. Who would believe me? I did not even believe me. I felt the anger well up inside me and I wanted to punch a hole through the wall. I had to figure it out. I picked up the phone and dialed Martha's number. She answered on the first ring and I got straight to the point.

"What do you know about black magic?"

"Mike, I don't think you want to go down that path and the only thing I can tell you comes from primitive cultures in the jungles of South America. I do know one thing. You have to believe me and let go of your need to battle what you consider this demon. You need to relax and remember what I told you earlier. Mike, I do believe you."

"Thanks, Martha," I said. "I will do my best. I'm sorry, I just am really scared and it's hard to pretend differently."

"Mike, this is only your fear. Have you ever read anything about *A Course in Miracles*?"

"No," I said.

"There are only two emotions: love and fear. Fear stands for 'false evidence appearing real.' This is not real, but in the absence of love, it will fool you. Just trust me, please."

"I do trust you," I said, and I hung up feeling as foolish and hopeless as I could ever remember. I felt badly for subjecting Caroline to this problem. I owed her my support. When I had spoken with her and held her in my arms, it had felt reassuring to be together, at least physically. If Lucy had used her so-called powers to break us up, in some ways she had also brought us together again. Caroline knew me, she loved me and, after all, wasn't that a slap in Ms. Black Magic's face.

Back in Connecticut, I had been lonely and worried about Mom. Lucy had not only listened, she had also appeared to understand how I felt. I wanted to know about my future and she had seemed so accurate in her assessment . . . until now.

"Boy did you get her number wrong." Caroline again reminded me when we next saw one another. "She will not stand in the way of 'us' and we need to commit to our relationship or she will be the winner."

I wondered what had just happened. Had I heard the "us" word paired with relationship? Did this mean we were back together? The pressure in my chest was really kicking into high gear. *Let it go*, I said to myself. *Just breathe in and out slowly like Martha told you to do. Surround yourself in white light and surrender.* I tried every back door approach that would take me to this loving place. But for the first time in my life, I could not go within. I was blocked from my highest source of love.

I could no longer stand by defenseless. Whatever it took, I vowed to confront this dragon within. I knew that dragons were legendary creatures that symbolized internal and external fear and that they were revered as spiritual creatures in some cultures. I also knew that our utmost terror was often caused by the uncertainty of what might happen. We shake in anticipation of the unknown or the imaginary reptilian beast that seeks to destroy us. This was not about the prince wielding his sword to triumph over evil. I was down to the bone afraid. I needed to make this "unknown" known. I would not surrender. As much as I feared taking action, I was more afraid of doing nothing.

In the weeks that followed, I learned what I could about black magic and how it worked. The occult was a far cry from a magician pulling quarters out of his sleeve. There was more written about casting spells than removing them and the remedies seemed as strange as the spells themselves. Surely this did not come down to finding a goat's heart and grinding up crow beak in a caldron. If knowledge meant power, I was looking in all the wrong places. This was not the type of discussion you could bring up casually at Friday night happy hour or even a topic about which you could solicit advice from close friends and family. The trusted few that heard our story suggested we seek professional help from a therapist or a minister—or, better yet, fly a witch in from Salem to counteract the spell. If only it could be that easy!

The unrelenting feeling of pressure in my head and chest finally convinced me to at least check it out medically. I made an appointment with an urgent-care facility hoping that I could remain incognito. I said nothing about what I thought it might be and stuck to the physical symptoms. After a barrage of medical tests, all which came up negative, and a thousand dollars of my own money invested, the best guess was that I was possibly depressed or suffering from anxiety. I was handed a courtesy referral to a psychiatrist and written a clean bill of physical health.

I started to lose clients, one by one. It would have been easy to rationalize that the excuses were all legitimate, but what was I giving off energetically? I knew it could not be good. Caroline and I were together only as a validation of the other's pain, like leeches sucking each other's blood for survival. I eventually decided that I had no other choice than to see the psychiatrist. I had visions of being institutionalized and lobotomized, like in *One Flew Over the Cuckoo's Nest*, but hoped a psychiatrist could figure it out without going to such extreme measures. I was surprised that Caroline did not support this and would not accompany me. I was never one to give up on an answer and leaving any stone unturned would have undermined my resolve. I decided I would lay it all out on the table during the first session. I spilled the beans inside of the first two minutes.

"I have been under the spell of a psychic who practices black magic and I need your help."

There was dead silence, so I kept on talking and spitting out my story. Finally I stopped, realizing there had been no more response other than the obligatory nod that let me know he was present in the room.

"What do you see?" I asked.

"I see that you are very upset about this," he replied. Then he sat back as if he had stated something other than the obvious.

Brilliant observation, I thought, but kept that thought to myself. We continued the session with nothing more brilliant than his initial comment coming from him in response to my story. Then, because I was desperate enough to continue doing what was not yet bearing fruit, we met for two more sessions. The only change I noticed from this work was a slight increase in my stress level because I was now another $400 further in debt.

It occurred to me that because this was not a mainstream problem, maybe I needed to go to another psychic, one who understood dark energy and could figure out how to counteract it. I remembered a client of mine raving about a psychic he had successfully consulted for a complicated personal issue and I asked him for the referral. I had not anticipated that she was in West Virginia, over an hour away, but it would be worth the trip if she could help me. The thought crossed my mind that I would be giving away my power to another psychic, but I questioned that I had any personal power left at this point. As long as she did not consult a crystal ball and tell me that Elvis had a message for me, I would listen.

The drive seemed longer than ninety miles. I meandered into rural countryside that seemed to deteriorate into abject poverty and finally reached a modest two-story house. It did not have a gaudy neon sign saying, "Psychic," a skull and crossbones, or any other type of occult sign, so I felt somewhat reassured. My heart was pounding as I rang the doorbell. I reminded myself to breathe, but I was beginning to resent simple prompts that did nothing to alleviate my stress. Of course I would breathe. Until recently, I hadn't ever been aware it was a choice.

The door opened slowly and only part way. I could only see her head.

"Hi, I'm Mike Gannon," I croaked.

"Oh yes, do come in," she said.

When the door opened all the way, what I saw made me wish I had not already identified myself. I wanted to say that I had the wrong address and run faster and longer than Forrest Gump. This woman was Quadruple X! I was shocked at the resemblance and mortified at the freaky reality that I was standing in the foyer of Lucy's plus-size twin. I followed her past the crumpled bag of Doritos on the floor, through a hallway that reeked of cat piss, and to her office, which was laden with clutter and crocheted doilies. I sat down, the blood totally drained from my head. She did not need to be a psychic to pick up on my discomfort.

"Is everything okay?" she asked.

"Sure, yeah, it's okay. I'm just nervous."

At least this time I was not paying $400 to establish that I was upset.

"No need to worry. Let's get to the reason for your visit."

"I believe I might have become a victim to dark forces or a spell of some sort."

I was not going to give her too much information this time. I wanted to apply some discernment and develop some trust in what she had to say.

"Well, let's take a look at that," she said as she leaned back in a caned-back chair that did not look sufficient to support her weight. "I see that we have a woman involved. Two actually."

I did not respond.

"They both have strong feelings for you and practice the arts."

"Which one?" I replied.

"Both," she said. "But one is very psychic and very powerful, I might add."

I wanted to ask, "Does she look just like you?" for clarification, but did not want to put her off, so I asked, "Can you tell me what is going on with me?"

"You are in a predicament with both of them. Can you tell me a little bit about each so I can get a better feeling for the situation? You *do* understand that they are in a power struggle for your attention, is that so?"

"I'm not sure. I thought Lucy was a friend of mine. We have been good friends for about six years."

Then, forfeiting my promise to keep quiet, I told her the whole story.

"Wow, I would say you got yourself in one heck of a mess!" she replied.

"So can you verify that what I am saying is true?" I asked, on the verge of begging for someone to believe me.

"Yes, to some extent I can," she replied.

I went straight for the kill. "I need to know how to get rid of this problem. What is the solution for this?"

I knew she saw my desperation and the sincerity in my eyes, which were now on fire with fear.

Her answer was immediate.

"I have no solution. I only wish I did."

My heart seemed to have stopped beating. I could not accept no for an answer.

"Well, have you ever dealt with anything like this before?"

"Not to this degree," she replied.

I resisted the possibility that, once again, I had dead-ended. I spent the next thirty minutes relentlessly searching for something she might discern that could help us unravel my predicament. I had already stayed much longer than my designated appointment time. The clouds hovering over the West Virginia hills were growing darker and not a ray of sunshine was left in the sky.

After accepting that nothing useful was going to result from this session, I drove home. I was angry and frustrated. Where was God in all of this? I felt like I was standing in front of a firing squad, helpless to save myself. I had endless questions but my questions only fueled more questions. As I was replaying in my mind what the psychic had told me, I recalled her saying that both women in my life practiced the arts. I had taken that to mean they were both psychic. Could she have meant both practiced black magic? I told Caroline about my meeting with the psychic. I thought she might want to know that the woman had validated our fear.

But she was angry and asked, "What if we can't break this?"

I looked at her with warrior-like determination and declared, "We *will* beat this!"

She did not respond and turned away with tears that I pretended not to see.

A week or so later, it was my thirty-third birthday and although I was in no mood to celebrate, Caroline insisted we go to a new Japanese steakhouse. At least sharing a table with others would prevent any tirades about our dilemma. The chef put on a spectacular performance with the usual knife throwing and egg flipping extravaganza. I could not help but notice that when the butter melted over the sizzling shrimp, I felt the same burning sensation in my chest. I refused to say a word about it because I had promised myself that I would not bring up the subject of psychic attack for any reason.

Dinner turned out to be enjoyable in a distant, unattached way. I was careful not to give off the "us" signal to Caroline. We were quiet at first on the way home. Then she launched into an unprovoked harangue about how much she hated Triple X. She had driven so I could imbibe on my birthday if I wanted to and within about ten minutes, her arm stiffened and she struggled to breathe. I grabbed the steering wheel while looking back and forth between the road and her.

"Caroline, what's wrong? Pull over and let me drive!"

Pain was written all over her face as it contorted into a left-sided grimace. I thought she was having a stroke. I could not panic and maneuvered the car from the passenger side off the road through three lanes of traffic. I ran around to the driver's seat, picked her up, and brought her around to the passenger's side. I got back in the car and drove like a mad person, heading towards the hospital.

"Caroline, talk to me!" I urged. I needed to keep her conscious. "Talk to me!" I tried to keep her focus.

Within a minute or so she seemed better. She refused to go to the hospital and explained what had happened. She claimed that the dark force had gripped her heart like a vice and when I asked how she knew that, she went into a rage claiming that I did not believe her. I took her in my arms and held her.

"I am so sorry," I kept saying over and over again.

I continued my search for people, books, or any kind of metaphysical and psychological methods that could shine light on this situation. I had no emotion left, none that I could feel. This was a losing battle, a bloodless fight that had no purpose, no reason, and no heart. How do you conquer an undefined enemy that has mastery over fear and encompasses you in a battle for which you are defenseless? I learned that in order to get a handle on something, the unknown has to first be made known. I pursued one path, only to find it dead-end, then another, and another. I never reached the center, never reached an understanding, and never found an answer. What was left for me was prayer.

> *God, if you can still hear me, know that I have not left you. I believe you have not left me. This depression or negativity will not stop me from finding my way back to you. Forgive me for choosing a path that would lead to this place of darkness. I ask for you to send me all the help you can to put an end to this and embrace me once again. I love you, I've always loved you, and I will fight for you. Please hear me.*

I waited to feel something, a twinge of hope, a flicker of light—any sign at all. Nothing.

One afternoon, as I watched the leaves from a tree fall to the ground leaving it naked and exposed to the winter, I wondered if the tree had any sense of anything or if there was any way it knew that it would have renewed life in the spring. It occurred to me that it did not need to know. Its renewal would happen anyway because it was a cycle of life and that was the way it was supposed to be. What was I to learn from that? Was this about acceptance of what is without resistance? Was this a test of some sort? Could it be there was no answer, and in that no answer, I would find peace? It sounded too bizarre, but what could have been more bizarre than what I had already experienced?

I ran the idea by Caroline. She shrugged her shoulders as if to say that she no longer cared. I dreaded ever having to tell my family about this but they knew something had changed and I owed them honesty no matter how much I hated to tell my story one more time. I decided to tell Brian so he could cushion it for Mom and Dad. I could not bear disappointing them. I thought about going to visit him in Atlanta, but I had no money to eat, let alone travel, so I called him on the phone.

"Brian," I said in my most positive voice. "Do you have some time to talk? I have something really important I need to tell you."

"Shoot!" he replied in his Cool Hand Luke tone.

"I've got something very screwed up happening to me and I don't know where to go or how to find the proper help for this kind of thing," I said.

"What are you talking about?" he asked sounding puzzled.

"Do you remember Lucy from Connecticut?"

"The pig?" he replied. "What about her?"

"Well, I think she might have done some weird psychic thing to me," I replied.

"Like what?" he asked.

"I don't know, some kind of curse," I said.

"What kind of curse?" he chortled, as if this was going to be the punch line to a bad joke.

"I've got this unknown, debilitating energy eating me up alive, and I don't know how to get rid of it," I said with enough desperation to take the chortle right out of him.

"Mike, what is wrong with you?"

"I don't know, but this is really happening!" I said.

"What is happening? Why are you being such a creep?"

Feeling helpless, I tried to go into greater detail, but I only dug myself in deeper and sounded as if I had just stepped off of Mars.

"I don't know what the hell you are talking about, but whatever it is, you need to get a grip!"

"Oh, thanks a lot! I have been going through pure hell with this situation and you are the only family member I have confided in. I hoped that you might at least listen without going off on me and all you can say is, 'Get a grip'?"

"That's about the gist of it."

"Sorry I called you. Thanks for all your help, not to mention your compassion, Brian. See you later."

Click.

I was crushed! With that response, I was certain to tell no one else in the family. For the first time since the crazy affair had begun, I cried. Actually, I didn't just cry, I totally lost it. I visualized choking the life from Triple X, breath by breath. I was more than angry, I was helplessly enraged!

I never knew whether Brian told our parents the story. Not one member of my family brought it up to me and I had no intention of finding out if they had been told. At this point, I envied the normal life. This depressive, negative energy wasn't something I could ignore, despite how far-fetched I know it sounded to others. I tried the psychiatrist route again and this time, at least, I was put on Zoloft for depression. It did nothing for the problem, but at least it somewhat lifted the doom and gloom of living with it. And I did feel a bit calmer. Maybe what I actually felt was numb, but at least it was some relief. One of my lowest moments throughout this ordeal was when my good friend Jake asked me to move out. He had never been the same after I told him about my problem. He never said but I could only speculate that he felt I was battling a bigger problem and he did not want me in the house. I did not blame him. I might have felt the same had our situations been reversed. I was sad because I knew it meant losing his friendship.

Homeless and with few funds, I moved into my office building, hiding every night until security had made their rounds. I had a small microwave and refrigerator and converted my futon from bed to chair each morning. I took my shower in the men's locker room. I had nowhere else to go. Caroline had managed to drift out of the picture and that was how I wanted it to remain. I had nothing much left to give and my life had taken a nosedive.

The one thing I didn't do was give up searching. I knew I would figure it out. I was fine physically and threw away the Zoloft. I stopped hating Lucy. I decided that whatever God had in store for me, he knew what he was doing, even if I had not figured it out. I skimmed through the pages of *Pathways* magazine, a local New Age journal, and read about a metaphysical trade show coming to the area. I decided to attend.

At the show, I went aisle by aisle with my antenna up, looking for answers. Then I spotted a familiar face. Was that Jeri who I had hypnotized for weight loss? I had been amazed by how quickly she had been able to go into a very deep trance. By the looks of her, it must have really worked. I walked over to get a closer look. She was with another woman and they were laughing about something. She recognized me immediately and introduced me to her friend Marilyn. We talked for a few minutes, joking about the strung out wacko behind us draped in a black banner announcing "End of Times" and selling survival kits.

"If you think some of this is weird," I blurted out, "you would never believe what has gone on with me."

Had I gone mad? I hardly knew Jeri. I knew that she was married to a doctor and had two teenage boys, but that was about it. What was I possibly thinking?

Then I said, "I would like to get together with you some time and catch up, and I will be sure to fill you in."

"Sure," she said. "That would be fun."

In that precise moment, next to a booth in which a tiny elderly lady claimed to talk to angels, I knew my life would be forever changed. I knew it in the same way the tree knew that after the long winter, spring would give it new life.

As I left the building, I randomly picked up a flyer that had fallen on my foot. It was for a book titled *The Dragon Doesn't Live Here Anymore*. I smiled.

That's right, he doesn't.

THE METAPHYSICAL SOAP OPERA

chapter 13

I did not sleep well that night, fraught with the anticipation that I was going to call Jeri and arrange a meeting. Whenever I applied logic to my strong gut feelings that Jeri could help me rid myself of the negative energy, I ended up spinning my wheels. The blatant truth was that I barely knew this woman. I sensed she could help me and I had read about individuals who could channel information from higher consciousness. With Jeri's remarkable ability to go into a trance, maybe it made sense that she could help. I vaguely remembered that she worked with victims of crime in preparation for trial, but I was not sure in what capacity. I needed to stop drowning in hopelessness and helplessness. I had decided that the dragon was moving out of my house, but now what?

By 11:00 a.m., she would have had enough time to return from the gym and I would call her then. I had formed the habit of going over conversations in my mind before they transpired and I did my mental run-through at about 10:45 a.m. I decided to leave the venue up to her. I dialed her number, mentally pleading that she would be home. I had trouble with leaving messages on answering machines because I could seldom hear the beep that prompted me to begin speaking. Just as I was ready to hang up, she answered.

"Are you still game to hear my crazy story?" I asked.

"Well, tomorrow would be good if you can come to my house. I will be stuck waiting for servicemen."

"I can swing by after my last morning client, around 11:45."

"Perfect," she said.

I offered to bring lunch, even though the thought of eating while telling my story forced my stomach to do handstands. Jeri graciously declined the offer saying she would be happy to fix something for me after acknowledging that she had bought a revolting cleansing diet at the trade show and had only one more day left of torture.

As I drove to her house the next day, I felt an energy shift as soon as I left the immediate vicinity where I lived. I left the frenetic energy of the cement high-rise jungle of office complexes to the peaceful expansiveness of open space. I felt a nostalgic connection as I passed the embankment of stately oaks where I would have turned off to go to our old house in Great Falls. I rarely saw any of my family these days. We all had separate households and Dad had a new cast of family members. I wondered how it had happened. How did such close attachments fade and new ones arise that had no prior family history? I swallowed hard and choked back resentment, reminding myself that this was no time to go down the dismal memory lane of disappointment. I needed to focus on the positive outcome of this meeting and fly on the wings of trust just one more time.

Reston was as beautiful as I had remembered. I approached Jeri's airy lakeside home, beautifully landscaped with a hint of oriental flair. The driveway plummeted sharply to a distinctively contemporary structure, which gracefully hugged the cascading shoreline. Jeri was her usual relaxed self as we sat in her breakfast nook overlooking the lake. Perched on her dock was a lone heron, oblivious to the flock of wild geese that had landed in the backyard. Suddenly I felt as if this creature represented how different I always felt, a strange bird that stood out, looking awkward and unlike the others. If I only belonged to that flock of geese, I could take wing and never have to tell my story again.

We had already exchanged the customary greetings and remarked on the weather being warm for November. We each gave a sketchy synopsis of what we had been up to for the last two years. Then Jeri launched right into it.

"So tell me Mike, what is up with you that could possibly be any stranger than the Armory full of bizarre vendors from the other day?"

I had hoped to ease into my story but she was ready to get right down to business. By this time I felt I could have recited my story in a drug-induced coma. I went through the entire ordeal: my association with Lucy and Caroline, all the help I had sought, and my inability to shake the negative energy I felt coming through my chest. I knew I would need to get to the point of my visit, so I ended my story by stating that I believed she could possibly help me.

Before I could foresee any reaction from her, she said, "May I ask why?"

"Just a feeling," I said. "In addition, I think your ability to access a trance state effortlessly would be invaluable."

"Would you mind if I ask you another really important question? Are you open to the possibility that this is your own creation?"

I paused, stunned.

"I'm not sure I know what you mean?" I fought back my usual defensiveness.

"I mean, do you believe that each of us create our own reality?" she asked.

"In what way?"

"Do you think we are responsible for what happens to us, and that it is not a matter of coincidence, bad luck, or wrong timing?"

She explained the reason she asked was that she had just finished reading the book, *The Celestine Prophecy*, which was based upon this premise and was one of the primary reasons she had attended the trade show.

"Mike," she said kindly, "I'm new to all of this, but I promise you I have no answers for you that you do not have within yourself. But my hunch is the same as yours: I might be able to help you get to the bottom of this. I do have experience preparing witnesses for trial, most of whom have been victims of violent crimes, and I can tell you I can be relentless with getting answers."

She started to explain that *The Celestine Prophecy* was an adventure novel based on a lost Peruvian manuscript. Although the story was fictional, it was a parable that described the ongoing spiritual evolution and the awakening of human consciousness to our individual and collective life purpose. Then the doorbell rang. Her two Persian cats, which had posed themselves as live art in one of the cutouts in the kitchen wall, scrambled over each other and ran upstairs. Jeri, in tandem, inadvertently kicked over the cats' bowl of water on her way to the door. The anticipated serviceman had arrived to inspect the heat pumps for the winter and also left a trail of soot from one room to the next. Jeri excused herself to clean up after him and I began wiping up the water that had splattered across the ceramic tile. Her fourteen-year-old son came into the room without my hearing him and found me squatting on the kitchen floor. The doorbell rang again before I had a chance to explain myself.

"Mom, it's the roof man," he shouted, "and there's another man on the kitchen floor!"

Jeri walked back into the kitchen, totally oblivious to the mayhem she had left in her wake and looking rather amused.

"Mike, I'm so sorry for the disruptions. It's just all happened at once. I usually live a far less disordered life."

We continued our conversation for a while and decided to meet again at my office.

"I will be happy to pay you for your time," I said, but she whisked me off with a definitive hand gesture.

"We'll work it out. Let's just see what transpires. Promise me one thing only," she said at the front door. "Buy the book and we can talk about it at our next meeting."

I left encouraged, even though I had no idea whatsoever where things were headed. As I drove away, I realized I was smiling, really smiling, for the first time in months.

The next day, on my lunch break, I visited the bookstore and marched up to the information desk.

"Excuse me. I'm looking for the book *The Celibate Prophet* or something like that." I found, to my embarrassment, that my deafness had once again misled me.

The haughty clerk sighed and puffed out her cheeks. *The Celibate Prophet?*" she hissed back. "Sir, are you referring to the number one bestseller, *The Celestine Prophecy?*"

"Sounds about right," I said.

Once I began reading this book, it was addictive; I could not put it down. It described how people manipulate energy fields and use them to control others. I knew it! This was Triple X. After two years of searching, there it was, right in front of me in writing, and Jeri had led me to it in the most casual and offhand manner. But as I read on, it began to make more sense as to why Jeri had questioned me as she had. According to this author, there are no coincidences or chance happenings. We create the situations that will draw in whatever we need when we are ready.

The following day Jeri came to meet with me at my office. I was exploding with so many insights from the book that I could not wait to share. God knows, I was ready. We began with a discussion of the book told as a fictional story, yet resounding with truth and an understanding of how spirituality affects our physical realm. Jeri shared how she had gone to a Catholic girls' school and felt the confines of organized religion far removed from any hint of spiritual enlightenment.

The best thing about Jeri was that she made me laugh. I liked the way she could insert humor into just about anything. For instance, she told me how she and her friend had put itching powder in the crotch of the nun's long underwear that was drying on a line behind the convent. I needed a good laugh and loved her stories.

I finally mustered up the courage to ask her if she knew anything about trance channeling. Other than radio and television channels, she had no idea. At least now, with our discussion of energy fields, I could explain it with more authority. As I had mentioned to her previously, I was fascinated with her ability to go into trance at a moment's notice. It was as if she had being doing it forever and she needed little prompting to access deeper states. I explained that although there are different forms of channeling, a trance channel was a person who could access a trance state and become a conduit for communication with higher consciousness. The voice itself is that of the channel but the content of the information or dialogue is often from outside his or her own personal realm or knowing. Many times another person will act as a facilitator and ask questions of the person channeling that will start the flow of information, as well as address the questions.

"This is the process I would like to try with you. Does it make sense so far?"

"As long as you don't think I'm going to talk to dead people and string plastic beads from my doorway."

I could tell that in spite of her own, zany demeanor, she wondered if I was going "a bit left of bubble," but she kept on listening.

"Would you be willing to try to see if anything comes up in trance? I can ask the questions," I said.

"I thought it was my job to ask questions," she answered. "But I'm willing to try."

"You're on!" I said.

I asked if I could tape the session.

"Fine, as long as you don't have me running around the room clucking like a chicken," she replied.

I grinned at the thought and promised no theatrics. I did not want to miss what was being said, and I knew I could have the tape transcribed if necessary. I asked her to close her eyes and relax by taking three deep cleansing breaths. I knew she did not need the induction process, but as a budding professional, I stuck with the protocol.

"I will be counting down from the number ten to one, and as I do, each and every time you hear my voice you will descend deeper and deeper into a hypnotic and relaxed state. Ten . . . going down to nine . . . as you hear my voice, you are feeling totally relaxed . . . eight and . . ."

Bingo! I knew she was already there, but I continued the descent. I went through the whole script about how she would be feeling safe and knew that at any time, should she choose to, she could open her eyes and be out of this hypnotic trance feeling fine.

"Now I am going to ask you to simply call upon the universe to take you to a place where you will bring in the highest energy, where you will be totally protected and open to universal wisdom. And when you reach that place, please signal by gently raising your right hand."

I flinched with the discomfort of acting on such a long shot that Jeri could access this state. I felt presumptuous and awkward. I held my breath in apprehension and within a few seconds, she raised her hand.

"Before you start," I said. "Could you be so kind as to identify yourself?"

I had suddenly remembered reading in a book on channeling to always identify the source of any information received.

Jeri began to speak.

"We have no identity as such. We are a part of the collective intelligence held in human consciousness. In a sense, we could say we are both of you. But we do not wish for you to attribute human embodiment and characteristics to this realm. We use the pronoun 'we' to accommodate your level of understanding in this communication."

Not that I understood, but I said, "Thank you." I then asked, my voice trembling a bit, "What is it that I need to understand or know to move forward and release this negativity?"

I had no idea how to phrase the request, so hoped it was okay. I waited no longer than a few seconds before she spoke.

"Michael has held back his own ability to move forward. His mind's eye will focus on what needs to be healed, but it will not do the work. He will know, but it is not in the knowing that healing takes place. For reasons of self-preservation, his ego self has split off from the spiritual. He has forsaken understanding for the temporary high of being right, or for reasons that defend the ramblings of the mind. There are many digressions on the path of spiritual enlightenment that arise from the ego. None are ever forced upon you. They come as the by-product of your own fear and ignorance. It is what it is."

I remembered thinking about that phrase at the trade show, about the tree losing its leaves, but I'd had no idea what it meant.

"Are you referring to the dark energy that I received from Lucy?

"Am I?" the voice replied.

"Are you not hoping to depend on what we say to solve your problems? Who has answers for you other than you? Who is responsible for your experience but you? You will say, with great resolve, that you have tried everything and this energy persists and you cannot make it go away. You will say you have asked God to intervene and yet, who has written the script for you?"

Not wanting to change focus, I asked a question instead of answering the one asked of me. "So just to clarify one thing, are you saying I am not under the spell of another?"

"Are you?"

I was beginning to feel like I was in a turnaround game, yet I was deeply awed by this presence.

"According to me, no! But I have a feeling according to you, yes."

"We have no say in this. Yes or no would be up for you to decide."

"So you are saying that no one has the power to hurt us? That we do it to ourselves?"

"That depends on your own belief. The answer is yes if you accept the pain that another inflicts upon you as your own."

"Okay then, is it possible for someone like a psychic to put a spell on me if I buy into the belief?"

"The flaw is in the question itself. You still hold the psychic responsible when you phrase it that way. Your thought about how she has power over you is your belief."

"Yes, but it feels like a dark energy coming from an external source into me," I replied. I was feeling anxious and confused. "It doesn't feel like it is coming from my thoughts."

"Who owns your thoughts and feelings? Would you rather believe she is in your body? Or are *you* in your body? And whose belief makes it dark? Your beliefs are made up of the thoughts that you hold to be true, so then who but you makes them true? You give your thoughts permission to form ideas that do not often serve your highest good. Does it serve you in any way to believe in darkness?"

"Of course not, but I would never choose to do this to myself."

"First, do not confuse choice with a selection off the menu of a mental process. Choice related to one's ego is that which creates the separation from your own source of creation or power."

"So ego is not a good thing?" I interjected.

"Is it?" they asked.

I was still confused, but I was beginning to see the picture. I was supposed to have the answers within me, but I was not sure how.

"I'm not fully sure I understand. How do I know I have the answers?" I persisted.

"But, indeed, you *do* know. Do you not see this is the very thinking that has gotten you into this? What is good or bad is determined by your beliefs about it. What makes something bad for you is based on your experience of it. But your experience of it is not who you are. Are you not more than the sum of your experiences? If you think the ego self is bad, then it will comply with your wishes. All of creation is one. Therefore, there can be no separation other than what the mind creates. Do you understand?"

My mind was going in a million circles.

"Is there more?" the source asked.

"Yes. I understand the concept of a medium who channels spiritual beings such as Seth, Michael, and St. Germaine. That's why I asked who you were. So then, could we say you are from God?"

"You could," they retorted, "or you could not."

And as quickly as "they" had entered, they disappeared.

I slowly brought Jeri out of the trance and back into full awareness. She opened her eyes and looked straight into mine.

"Do you know what just happened?" I asked, barely able to contain my excitement.

"Not really, but one thing I know for sure, I can assure you that what came out of my mouth and from my voice did not come from anything I personally know. One thing I do know, very similar to the legal arena, they certainly can put any question back on you faster than my grandmother flips pancakes. Also, do you remember last week when I told you to read *The Celestine Prophecy*, and for whatever reason, I asked if this might be your own creation? I have absolutely no idea why I would have said such a thing. I haven't told you how badly I felt when I first asked that question. I know I was not in a trance then, but could I have been channeling and was unaware of it?"

I looked at her with a smile on my face and asked, "Could you?"

We both roared with laughter.

"This is big. How can I ever thank you enough? Right now I am so overwhelmed, I don't know what to say. How about I buy you lunch? I'm starved," I offered.

"Me too!" she said.

I grabbed my keys and we left.

Just as I turned to lock my office door, I saw that Caroline was right behind me. I had not seen her in months.

"Hi," she said timidly, brushing past Jeri. "I'm here to take you to lunch."

"Caroline, I have a meeting right now," I said and abruptly turned my back on her.

I left her standing, jaw dropped to the floor. As Jeri and I walked down the hall, I could almost feel Caroline mentally checking out everything Jeri was wearing. I knew that trouble was looming on the horizon.

Once we got into the car, Jeri said, "I take it from your coolness that was 'the' Caroline?"

"You are right on," I smiled. "I apologize for not introducing her, but the less was said, the better.

"Why would she show up now? Do you see what I mean? This is like some kind of curse. How could she have possibly timed it at this moment when I'm making progress to end it all?"

"Stop," Jeri said firmly. "Caroline is responsible for Caroline, and if she shows up unannounced, whose problem is it?"

"Hers," I replied. "Thank you for making me aware of that. Now I will choose to see it differently."

"Do you now know that you are responsible for her getting it this time so she doesn't return?"

I nodded affirmatively as we headed out of the parking lot and into the busy afternoon traffic.

Before the day was finished, Caroline made a follow-up call to let me know how rude I was for leaving her in the dust. It was time for me to come to terms with my relationship. Saying good-bye did not mean until next time, it meant for good. It had to be a clean break, which meant no lingering friendship or open doors that would let her hold onto the illusion that one day we would reignite the flame. As she continued to talk, I tuned her out and when we hung up, I knew what I needed to do.

I imagined her reading a letter in which I said good-bye and asked her not to contact me again. I instantly felt her sadness and then the anger that always followed with her. I had encountered this reaction so many times I was ready for a different ending. In my mind's eye, I saw her vow to herself that she would never speak to or think of me again. I felt a cold shiver come over my body. It felt right. I needed to visualize this for myself as well. I had to accept responsibility for my part in allowing the relationship to continue. Saying good-bye was only the first step. It was important to let go of the memories and associations because I knew they had a way of resurfacing as future triggers.

I saw myself get up, walk down a long path, and say good-bye to everything she had represented along that path: Saturday nights curled up in bed, picnic lunches along the Potomac, Friday nights at the movies, long talks about our future, and most of all, a dream that would never come true. When I came to a big clearing and could see for miles, I knew my time with her had ended. I imagined hugging her with tears streaming down my face. In honoring the parts of our relationship that I treasured, I could be grateful for the experience and let it go in a loving, rather than resentful, space. The mistakes, the pain, and the frustration were behind me. Letting go, even if it was a gesture offered in visualization, had the power to set me free.

I also followed up with the action that would uphold my visualization. I wrote a heartfelt letter to her that night. I was kind and grateful for the time we had spent together but I did not wish to include her in my future. I asked, as straightforward and lovingly as I possibly could, that she never contact me again. (To her credit, she never has, nor have I seen or even run into her again.) I could see how endings were the opening to new beginnings.

The next few times Jeri and I met, we were still amazed at what had happened. She rarely spoke about herself directly, only in passing. She had definitely perfected the art of being "other oriented." The voice continued to speak through her and we spent many afternoons enthralled in the teachings presented to us, pages upon pages spilling into one notebook after the other. We touched upon universal truths and insights. We kept trying to understand the bigger purpose. I wanted to make sure that it was not all about me. Jeri posed many questions of her own. I suggested she write down any questions she might have so I could ask them for her during our sessions.

I had some difficulty figuring out what Jeri really thought about channeling, so one afternoon I decided to ask her directly.

She said without hesitation, "Mike, I don't have any prior beliefs about it, as it pertains to me. It is new enough in my realm of experience that I don't have any judgments about it. I do feel that it would take a very large change in our present consciousness to embrace or adapt to another way of thinking. And even as I say this, I can hear them say, 'This is nothing but an illusion about another belief.' I feel overwhelmed with the possibility of repatterning collective thoughts and emotions."

As if she wanted to remove herself from the line of inquiry, she asked, "Mike, how willing are you to go back and change your thoughts about the trauma that has occurred in your life?"

"I am open to anything at this point."

"Good!" she exclaimed. "I know everyone wants a method, scientific proof, credible resources, and on and on. What if we throw out all credibility and caution to the wind and rely on our inner selves? I have just one more question. Is it possible that when

I go into a trance and you ask the questions, I could be receiving collective information available through my higher self?"

We both said in unison, "Could it?"

"I have to be honest with you Jeri, I can't bring in this information on my own yet like you can, so I don't know how helpful I'm going to be in this process of tuning into a higher source."

"I want to say something about you, Mr. Michael James Gannon. You are a remarkable human being and I am in admiration of what you have accomplished in your life. You have pushed yourself to do things that other deaf people would never consider. Sure, you said your parents would not allow you to be brought up in a deaf world and good for them, but you had to do the work. You had to face the adversity. I can't even imagine what it would be like to go to school and not hear and have to take notes from lip-reading. You graduated from a top-notch university, started your own business, and the thing that is most endearing about you is you care about people. So if you really don't know how helpful you will be, we aren't leaving here until you figure it out."

Although amused at her tenacity, I knew she meant it. I explained to her about the place in my mind where I would go to live out my dreams, where no one would judge me, and where I could be, do, or have anything I wanted. I was always happy there and anything was possible. I would feel it, be and believe in it, and then I would play it out, over and over again. The funny thing was that many times it would really happen just like I envisioned it.

For example, I would see myself getting an "A" on a test knowing full well it was going to be next to impossible, but I would not accept the impossibility of it. Because I was very visual, I could see the actual "A" written on my paper, and I would imagine my parents congratulating me. I would imagine all the details and live them, again and again. I expected them to happen and although they didn't always happen as I envisioned, I still thanked God because I figured he was listening and he heard what I wanted.

When I was a child, I thought this place I retreated to was a special place for deaf people like myself to go and daydream. As I became older, I shifted more from a thinking mode into actually feeling what was happening in my imagination. At times, I didn't want to leave. So in a nutshell, that was my own version of a trance.

With tears in her eyes, Jeri said, "Mike, I think we both are crossing the threshold into unknown territory, so let's just stay open and see where it goes."

We both knew we had been brought together for a reason, but we did not speak about it other than to marvel at what had happened. For the next several weeks, we addressed some of the core issues and thinking that had attracted the aberrant, negative energy into my life. Without any formal training, Jeri's intuitive abilities masterfully guided me back to the memories, feelings, and wounding that had not yet been acknowledged or felt.

She began with Mattie. "I want to you to go into a relaxed state where you are feeling safe and take some deep breaths."

I was already trained in self-hypnosis and was able to induce a relaxed state even with my eyes open part of the time, which enabled me to lip-read.

"Go to the day that Mattie died and let me know when you are there."

I brought up the memory instantly. I had replayed it in my mind so many times. I gestured with my hand, acknowledging that I was there.

In that same instant, she said, "Mike, in this moment, stop the story and put it in freeze mode."

I must have looked confused, but she kept right on going.

"Now I want you to drop out of your head and go into your heart, to the place in your body where you feel the pain. And when you are there, let me know."

When I acknowledged I was there, she then asked, "Now tell me what you see right now?"

"I'm in the moment when Dad told me Mattie had died."

"Okay, bypass the details of what happened and get into the feeling."

"Jeri, I'm not sure what you want me to do? How can I feel the pain without remembering what happened?"

"Memory is a function of the brain. Go to your heart," she replied.

I could feel my resistance coming up, and told myself to just focus on the feelings.

"You're doing just fine. It's okay Mike. Just allow your breath to take you to that place in your body where you can feel the pain. Breathe into the pain and allow it in. Let me know when you can feel it."

I breathed in air, allowing a defenseless, vulnerable feeling to break through the raw pain of his death.

"I need to say the words," I croaked, hardly able to speak.

"You are resisting the feeling Mike. Go to the pain and don't retell the story."

I could not go there. It was as if I was making a cadaver of myself, complete with rigor mortis, defying the flow of life within me. The process was going nowhere.

I was just about to give up when Jeri said, "It's okay, Mike, let me tell the story."

I was in my mind enough to know she had no idea what had happened that day, only that my little brother had died when I was about nine. She relaxed her voice and began speaking from the place of collective consciousness. I could always recognize the shift.

"Your mom and dad have just walked into the room and you can see that Mattie is not with them. Your heart sinks because you can tell that something is wrong. Stay focused on your heart, Mike."

She continued, telling what had happened with amazing accuracy and detail. I followed her words and calming tone, choking back sobs until I could hardly breathe. Hurt grabbed hold of my throat. I felt my helplessness spinning out of control.

"Mike, your mother was not in the room. She had left to go upstairs. How did that make you feel?"

"It was the most incredible feeling of abandonment," I said.

"Go to that place of feeling and stop the story."

I wondered how she knew that my mother had gone upstairs.

"Feel it now," she insisted.

I did as she asked. And I recognized that the feeling had lingered with no consciousness of time. It was a shadow that had hovered over me for as long as I could remember, something like an underlining depression with a low, vibrating hum. I wondered why it had accompanied me for so long.

"Now I want you to let go of this experience and release it from your body," she said.

I knew that releasing the experience was long overdue and, to my amazement, I could feel it leave. I needed no words to release it. I stayed in feeling mode.

"When you're ready," she said, "I would like you to come back to the present moment where we are in this room."

I opened my eyes and glanced at her, not knowing what had just emerged. I did know that a new light had been shed on an old, sunken ship anchored deep down in the murky waters of the forbidden place called feeling. I needed to move, I needed fresh air, and I needed to breathe.

"Good job Mike!" she said. "I'm going to go now and I don't want you to go back to the story, only to the feeling." She squeezed my hand and left me to just be, sensing that I needed to be alone.

I decided to take a walk. I had realized I needed to take the time to look further into this repressed trauma and see if there was more to uncover and release. I knew I needed strength to get through whatever hidden pain awaited me, so I said a little prayer. "Dear God, I don't know how much of this hurt is still buried deep down inside of me, but I trust this is what I've needed to do to move forward and away from darkness. I ask for the strength and courage to handle as much as I can."

I walked to a place far away from the high-rise office building I called home. I sat by a pile of discarded construction debris left over from yet another building that had not yet been finished. I, too, felt like unfinished business. It was no coincidence that I chose this spot.

I slowly opened the feelings that still lingered around my brother's death and dropped down into my heart. I practiced the plummet from head to heart multiple times.

I was fascinated to be able to feel the shift. I could feel my emotions coming to the surface much like a tsunami. With little warning, the waves of emotions were coming up and gaining strength.

The timid voice of a frightened inner child screamed within. Nothing was going to hold back the flood of tears crashing into consciousness. When they hit shore, their power and force subsided.

As I walked back to my home almost an hour later, I had to look at myself for the first time and own the responsibility. I had used my mind to revictimize myself with the pain by retelling the same story over and over again. I had kept it alive inside. I had not felt the pain and let it go after that life-altering moment. Instead, I had waged my own war within.

"When our repressed wounding goes unaddressed, it allows our shadow selves to *attract* more darkness," Jeri had said. She had explained how difficult it could be to open the core wounding that has been pushed down and suppressed for so long. Through the repetitive process of denying our own pain, we tend to develop an emotional pattern of protection as a mechanism for survival. That pattern becomes ingrained over time and although I was consciously ready to deal with the issues of my past, it would not change my currently ingrained pattern without the basic understanding of what I had created.

I had been taken aback by Jeri's understanding of these principles and how her carefully constructed questions had enabled me to find answers for myself. When I asked her how she had learned to do this, her reply had been that she understood that victims of crime often hold on to pain as a way of feeling in control. And she reminded me that I had invited her to help me.

Jeri would never have been mistaken for the Mother Theresa type and she would have been the first to tell you so. Her association with this newly acquired spiritual path was kept totally to herself—with the exception of friends like me. She was funny and a great storyteller who could captivate an entire room. Her ease in finding clarity with what had transpired reminded me of windshield wipers clearing off a mud-smeared window. I no longer felt like I was being kept in the dark. It seemed that the way out was to be open to the answers that were being elicited through the questions asked from within. I accepted that every day of my life offered a choice to begin again and was beginning to understand that it is the negativity of yesterday that chains us to the past.

There was so much for Jeri and me to learn as neophytes on this new spiritual path. We decided that we would enroll in spiritual classes offered by a small local, holistic, nondenominational church. Jeri excelled as a student of metaphysics and she enrolled in a nondenominational ministerial program geared towards spiritual psychology, which would enable her to do counseling. I was no longer standing before a great door of change begging entry. I had been invited in to participate in a bold new spiritual frontier that challenged the boundaries of traditional beliefs.

My business started to pick up again and I was getting back to the old me. I forgave Brian for his insensitivity, even though we never had a conversation about it. I realized he could not possibly understand what I did not even understand myself and I should have stopped expecting him to show compassion long ago. He moved up from Atlanta to Virginia after his business failed and I was hopeful that we would reconnect as adults.

Brian and I found an apartment to share and I was able to move out of hiding in my office dwelling. Just as both Brian and I were getting back on our feet, Dad appeared on our doorstep after his second marriage failed. He was jobless, depressed, homeless, and broke. This was far from being a jubilant reunion of the Gannon men. Brian wanted nothing to do with Dad and made himself as scarce as possible. I was a softer hit, spending time with him and trying to help him out of his misery.

Unfortunately, he would not budge to help himself. Day after day he refused to get up from the couch. He wallowed in self-pity and alcohol during the day, and then visited a local bar in the evening. He was still a good-looking man and knew how to work a crowd. Within months, he met a woman and moved in with her. I was subjected to Brian's "I told you so," but I was glad we had given him kindness and a fighting chance to stand on his own. I liked this woman and felt she would be good for him. Brian insisted it would not last. So it was back to the two of us once again and I saw little of him.

I was beginning to feel lonely and dated off and on. I reminded myself that until my emotions were healed and I was back on track, it I would be like knocking the scab off a wound and starting the healing process all over again. Maybe I would turn out to be the "Celibate Prophet" after all.

Jeri and I continued to meet regularly. She monitored my progress and held me accountable. She had mastered a skill similar to channeling called "automatic writing." It was a process that would be initiated after she stated an intent regarding a question, a clarification of something already covered, or some entirely new train of thought. Without any forethought, she would write without stopping or lifting her pen until the message was complete. It was a different process than me asking the questions. Wisdom flowed like a fresh mountain stream many times totally unsolicited and often illegible, which was very uncharacteristic for Jeri because the nuns had demanded perfect penmanship of her during her days in Catholic girls' school.

I poured over these writings and organized them into categories. Somehow I knew we would be referring to them for quite some time. We made no claims of prophecy, or sacred writing, or the discovery of profound truth. We used them in everyday living because they made such incredible sense about life, emotion, thought, and spiritual growth. They moved us to a place of greater contentment and as Jeri continued with her practice, she helped many others find this same peace of mind.

I understood how my feelings of hopelessness and vulnerability perpetuated my negativity. I had built an armor of protection that imprisoned my own fear. God patiently waited to come in at my front door. I invited him in but then gave him no space to enter until I was ready to let go of the fearful emotions that blocked the presence of love. I now understood that this was how a powerful negative energy survived. The hurt and pain were perpetuated through repetition. Hurt and pain begot more hurt and pain. Old feeling arose and spilled over into the present, robbing me of joy.

As much as I was able to grasp and incorporate this information into my life, I still sought further clarification on how I had managed to have all the right characters in place and how I had convinced myself that I had been psychically attacked. Once I had done the work of change, the answer was given in the simplest of terms. Jeri again allowed the wisdom to flow, this time onto paper.

"Obviously, you did not sit down by yourself and write this metaphysical soap opera. You allowed others to write the script for you. You only participated in reenacting the drama. Allow us to explain. When Lucy first told you that she had put a curse on her boyfriend, you felt the need to protect yourself and held on to the fear. You confided that fear to Caroline, allowing her to attach to the same fear. So you both energized it. However, do not forget that in this triad, Lucy told you this information about spells to induce fear in you because you had not given her the attention she wished. Your entire casts of characters were all perpetuating the same fear and the same story about the spell. This is called collective energy.

"Thus far nothing has outwardly transpired. However, when a thought, belief, or an idea becomes collectively energized within the subconscious mind, it opens the doorway for the conscious mind to do the same. If you collectively believe in this power, you give it more fuel. Think about it. Caroline wanted you at all cost, attracting physical symptoms that she could attribute to Lucy having this hold on you. Remember, the body plays the fear game as well. You developed physical symptoms to protect yourself from a relationship with Caroline because you held on to the wound in your subconscious memory that she would hurt and leave you again.

"In the interim, you continued to ignore Lucy, so this fed into her fear and anger and she used what she believed has dark power. So in essence, all of you were buying into the same premise. You went on a desperate search to end it, only you intensified the fire with all of your collective thoughts and energy feeding into the cauldron of boiling fear and negativity. Caroline guilted you into signing up for another relationship round with her. Then your fear was even greater because if you did not stop this hold, she would leave you again and again, on and on.

"But, it did not stop there. You brought in the wonderful lady from South America who had the most reasonable advice, but then reverted to another psychic and a psychiatrist who suggested that you needed drugs. What an exciting episode of *As the World Turns*. Just turn on the afternoon soap operas if you want to validate your story.

"We all have belief systems, which interact individually and collectively to play out the drama. Now your question might be, are these things true? Are they? Well, for you they are. For example, someone else might have thought Lucy was a terrible psychic, which in your experience was not true. Lucy, however, might have believed this man she practiced black magic on was her boyfriend. Maybe the boyfriend had not considered himself to be her boyfriend at all. So does that make what she thought untrue? Do you see? It is your perception that you label as truth. Your judgments support the thoughts and give you back what you put out. So the more you believed she had a hold on you, the more evidence you drew in to support that conclusion and, thus, your cast of characters to act out the parts with you."

I must have looked like I had run face first into a truck.

Jeri said, "Mike, you don't have to absorb this all at once. It's okay. As humans, this is what we do."

I started in with the "what-if's."

"Jeri, what if I had never met you to interrupt this? What if I had not figured this out on my own?"

"Stop kicking yourself and second-guessing what might have happened. You got it, now move on!"

Jeri could be counted on to be as direct as high noon.

"Now, here is the part I think you will like," she said. I could tell she was excited as she shuffled through her handwritten paperwork. "Here goes. There are universal laws that govern our universe that always apply and they have been described in different ways throughout time, but they are based on the fact that everything in the universe is comprised of energy. We are all connected to that energy by our thoughts, words, feelings, and by what we believe. Okay, we're clear on that much?

"Here is the part that pertains to you. From what I have learned about the universal law of attraction, I have this hunch that you were innately born knowing how it works and have applied it your entire life. Do you remember telling me about the God sound and how you could hear this vibration even though you were deaf? Not to get off the track, but there is also the law of vibration, which states that every thought and feeling has its own sound vibration, or frequency.

"Okay, it gets better. When you would go into that space, you would become anything you chose and you would make up situations and play them out in your mind—and then you would see them happen in real life. Well guess what? That was no coincidence. That was the law of attraction. Every human being has the ability to be, do, and have whatever he or she wants; they just need to know how to attract it. You did!"

"What? Say that again," I said, feeling like Simple Simon.

"You experienced, from a very young age, what most people at this very moment do not know the first thing about consciously. We have the ability to attract what we want when we feed it with our thoughts and feelings. You do that all the time."

"That's for sure. It's what got me into this mess with negative energy."

"Yes Mike, but it also works the other way around when you feed it with positive energy. Don't you see? Those daydreams were more than just an idle pastime. Don't get me wrong. There is more to this and it is not a magic carpet ride. Just like all the negative stuff with Lucy, it works in both directions. Do you understand how big this is? I started reading about it in a class on spiritual psychology and it made me think of some of the stories. So I reverted to my automatic writing to see what else, if anything, I could understand about this."

She had earmarked a page she wanted to share with me.

"One day, you and Mike will be capable of moving mountains of information should you choose. You are not only scribes, but you will show by example what great things are possible to those who will believe in themselves as creators of their own reality. To those who are able to accept this new paradigm of belief in the next millennium, anything is possible."

In my moment of speechless overload, I poured us both a glass of wine. I could be a scribe? I hated to write.

It was late by the time I walked Jeri to her car. This had been an eye-opener in many ways, but it had left me dazed. We were both energized. Not in my imagination nor in my God space, but in the blackened sky above me, I saw a shooting star descend as if it were deliberately heading straight towards us.

"Did you just see that?" I yelled.

"If we needed a visible sign from the universe," she said, "I think that little bit of razzle-dazzle might just do the trick."

I awakened the next morning to a different light—within and around me. I had surrendered to the darkness and had not closed my eyes until the sun poured its radiance into my bedroom window. I was free. I was back home where I belonged.

FROM THE KINGDOM WITHIN

Despite the perceived spiritual awakening on our planet, believed to be New Age thinking, mainstreamers—at least in the Washington, DC area—were paying little attention. Channeled information did not exactly fall into the class of "Acceptable Beliefs 101" with this more conservative base. It seemed that we had hurdles to jump before we might convey this type of communication with any sense of credibility. Sharing this experience amidst raised eyebrows reminded me of the judgments I had already encountered in my life and somewhat blemished my enthusiasm to stretch those limits.

It fascinated me how some information in any spiritual tradition became accepted and other thinking disregarded. As a little boy, I trusted that my invisible guardian angel stood guard at night while my hearing aids were off. Other kids held the distinct advantage of being able to hear the monster lurking in the closet. There was no telling who could have crept into my room. They could have brought in a marching band without my having heard it. When I was told that my own special angel would protect me,

I had compelling reasons to believe it. This was acceptable faith-based belief.

I knew that depending on where you lived in the world, and even in this country, the prevailing belief systems framed the receptivity of the message. The recognition of prayer as one-way communication was an accepted religious practice where I live. If it was alleged to be a two-way dialogue, it sent the believability factor plummeting, despite the long held tradition in both Christianity and Judaism of two-way dialogue with the divine.

I often felt like a neophyte craving the promise of living in a totally new paradigm. These insights given to us resonated with a personal and unshakable truth and were not predicated on anyone else's approval. I believed what we were receiving, but I was not sure I was ready to share those insights with the rest of the world. My own experiences of connecting to higher consciousness did not fit my own traditional background, but I was more than willing to remain open. This meant foregoing the safety net of acceptance. I had jumped before. I could jump again.

I was determined to learn as much as I could about this new shift in thinking that burst the lid off my life. I enrolled in an advertised seminar that offered an alternative approach to increasing wealth and abundance. It was far from Wall Street worthy, but I twisted Jeri's arm to join me. We made our way through the DC evening rush hour to a facility housed in a rundown neighborhood. This did not exactly exude a sense of abundance, but I was determined not to allow any outside influence dissuade me.

A very petite and attractive woman somewhere in middle age greeted us with great exuberance. After the customary introductions, she clasped her hands together in excitement and raised her voice a few notches in utter delight as she announced the first group exercise. She asked us to remove our largest bill from our wallet and scanned the room to make certain that everyone had followed instructions. Jeri flashed me one of her wisecracking looks, as if the woman were preparing to execute a robbery.

Then, as if she were asking us to do something within the realm of everyday behavior, the woman requested that we each spend a few moments smelling our money. I sat in the first few rows in order to lip-read, and decided that I must have missed a few words and misconstrued the instructions. Evidently not! Everyone around me began gingerly sniffing his or her bill. She further suggested we integrate all of our sensory awareness to evoke a "oneness" and feeling of connection with our money. I did not dare glance over at Jeri because I knew that the amused look on her face would set me off. I kept my eye on my bill as we tripped off to La-La Land.

I could feel the instructor's intensity as she explained that this was a process of focused intent. She asserted that, for most of us, our beliefs about money were either centered on the lack of it or on it being dirty in some way. She noted that we have been instilled with the idea that we should maintain secrecy around our finances, told that it is undesirable to love money because it is the root of all evil, and bombarded by relentless attention to the woes of poverty, greed, theft, and countless other negative aspects of finance. She stated that the currency we held in our hands was only a medium of exchange that represented our ability to have what we want. She believed that when we hold money in the highest regard and feel love, we shift our perception. Further, by using our senses and emotional center in a positive way, we could change our thoughts and attract a more favorable relationship with wealth. Conversely, if our relationship with money was adversarial, then we were coming from negativity and would attract more negativity.

I felt a more comfortable sense of purpose that night within myself, despite the money sniffing. I had not clamored to write notes or obsess about what I might have missed. This was the beginning of a new relationship with my own thoughts and it needed to be positive.

When I dropped Jeri off that evening, I asked, "So, are you one with the money?"

"I *am* the money," she chuckled as she jumped out of the car.

"You are looking pretty green to me," I replied, and drove away before I could see her "you are such a geek" look that often trailed my puns.

I returned home and immediately pulled out my old physics textbook from college. I had remembered that energy of a similar quality and vibration attracts the same, but I could not corroborate that this specifically included thoughts and emotions. I concluded that energy was energy despite the form we assign to it. I closed the book and headed back to the kitchen to rummage through the refrigerator. I looked around my condo and noticed that despite the dim, forgiving light streaming from a streetlight, our furniture looked old and worn out. Brian and I had haphazardly comingled our belongings, most of which were not even junkyard worthy. Ever since the Brian/Dad standoff, the household tension between Brian and me was palpable. Our lease was within weeks of being up and the rent increase we would endure if we signed another lease was an act of blatant piracy. It was time for me to move on.

I crawled into my bed and, as always, removed my hearing aids. My mind was still reeling from the seminar. I did not exactly embrace the practice of "bill sniffing," but I did go to that silent place in my mind where my visualization included all of my senses. Like Jeri had said, just maybe my make-believe world was really an inner knowing that I could attract what I wanted in my life. Why not start with where I lived?

I closed my eyes and imagined a condo that was well appointed, comfortable but elegant, masculine but not macho. I used the view of Jeri's lake as the backdrop for my new home and visually designed my space and furnishings. I must have drifted off to sleep imagining my new queen-size bed draped with a down comforter to keep me warm. I woke up energized the next morning and, strangely, not at all unhappy that I was still sleeping on the same beaten up mattress with the same worn out faded green blanket. What had changed was the absolute knowing that I would find the perfect place and then draw it into my life.

I decided to enlist the aid of a real estate agent to find a privately owned condo that I could lease with an option to buy, rather than deal with another rental complex. The very first place that appeared on the market was only about a mile from where Jeri lived. The trees were in full bloom and it was one of those welcomed no-humidity days in the 70s. I would love living in this community. I agreed to meet with a real estate agent in the adjacent shopping complex. She was a pleasant woman, but extremely chatty. She chattered on as we walked along the sidewalk to the condo. I had not noticed much about the immediate surroundings because I had been concentrating on reading her lips. When she opened the front door to the unit, which had its own outside entrance, I was literally blinded by the sun beaming into the room. The minute I focused my gaze, I realized that the sparkling in front of my eyes was a lake glistening like glass. I had not heard her say that the lake was literally in my backyard. I stood there, totally transfixed, as several ducks glided past my view, with the orchestrated precision of an act in Cirque du Soleil. I had seen them in the visualization of my new surroundings and now they were before me.

"I'll take it," I said immediately.

"Well you haven't even seen it yet," she said.

"I don't need too," I replied.

She did not know that I had already claimed it from within; it belonged to me. The morning after I moved in, the ducks reappeared and paused in front of my balcony as if to welcome me.

As I decorated my new place, I plunged into the concept of accepting my ability to create my reality without regard for a reality check of my finances. I opened a credit card account and decorated to the hilt. I skipped the down comforter in deference to the ducks, but nothing else was spared. One afternoon Jeri and her husband, Jack, stopped by to help me with some of the finishing touches. We were hanging my most recently purchased artwork, the perfect touch for the space over my sofa. I felt especially pleased with myself because I had successfully negotiated with the gallery for a much better price. Jeri was clearing away the coffee table so we could view the full effect. She handed me the invoice and certificate of authenticity to file away.

"Has your inner creator envisioned who is going to pay off your credit card?" she asked. She was flippant, but I could sense an element of concern.

"No," I said, hesitating and starting to feel a bit uneasy but attempting to defend my manic spending spree.

"Cheer up Mike. I have a $100 bill you can sniff."

"Very funny," I retorted, knowing full well she had a valid point.

Her husband, Jack, was accustomed to her boldness and immediately changed the subject from the personal matter of my debt. He questioned whether the artwork was hanging perfectly level on the wall.

Did I truly believe that I was going to attract the money from the ether? Mom always told us that money didn't grow on trees. I knew fear was my worst enemy and would return more of the same, but how could I dismiss the uncertainty I was feeling? Decorating my home did not exactly fall in the category of spiritual priority, especially with the emphasis on the material aspects of my vision. Jeri could sense that my mood had changed and tried her best to cajole me into a better frame of mind.

"How about we go for a financial consult with higher consciousness?" she suggested, trying to resurrect my sense of humor. I was ready and quick to accept the offer.

"Will tomorrow work?"

"It will," she replied.

It was barely 9:00 a.m. the next day when she arrived. As always, we sat directly across from one another, this time at my new glass dining room table. We assumed our roles, Jeri as the receiver and me as the questioner. Jeri began to speak, as she always did, from a place so different from her everyday demeanor.

"You ask to seek truth, yet the truth is before you. How can we be of assistance?"

"I am confused that my ego is causing me to act irresponsibly with my finances."

"Do you question your creation, or not having the money to pay for it?"

"Both I guess."

"Is that a guess or an answer?"

"I'm not really sure."

"Well let's start with what makes you unsure."

"I suppose it might have been foolish to have racked up a big credit card bill to get this place decorated."

"And what has changed in the now?"

"I really do not have the money to pay for it."

"Do you want to have the money to pay for it?"

"Of course, but I don't."

"That's right, you don't."

I was beginning to feel frustrated. "Yes, that is my problem. I put it on the card because I couldn't pay for it outright."

"Has any creditor been knocking on your door asking for the money?"

"No," I answered.

"Do you expect them to come tonight? Tomorrow maybe?"

"No, not really!"

"So then, what you are saying is that you are willing to give up this present moment of joy and split yourself off from your creation, all because a moment of fear stole your attention."

"Well, I was trying to be accountable for my actions."

"What actions?"

"Spending money I did not have?"

"Is that bad?"

"It can be."

"Well, is it bad right now?"

"It is, if I am not able to pay the bill."

"Where do you feel bad?"

"In my conscience, I would say."

"Is that a part of your body?"

"Well, no, it's more in my mind."

I was growing weary of the turnaround format.

"I assume you are referring to the thoughts you are having as being in your mind?"

"Yes, that would describe it."

"So whose thoughts are they?"

"They are my thoughts."

"But the bank has not come yet today have they?"

"No."

"Well then, why do you allow these thoughts to cause fear over what has yet to happen? Do you see where this is going? You are creating a story about what might happen and allowing it to ruin the happiness of this beautiful creation."

"Yes," I said.

"Do you really believe that?"

"To some extent," I replied.

"To the extent that you do not, this state of mind continues to brew negative thoughts. Do understand that these thoughts have equal ability to attract what you do not want. They are as magnetic as the positive ones."

"I suppose that would make sense," I said, trying to not feel irritated.

"So then, why do you do it? How does the fear of not paying

off your credit card serve you along with your strong belief system that debts are bad? For you, the very act of accruing debt tells you, 'I am unable to pay for my purchases.' Is this not so?"

"Well of course it is so."

I had put the positive energy into seeing my place with beautiful things and had attracted that into being, but I had also congruently put into motion the fear I held about debt. It seemed so logical in retrospect. And just as rapidly as the conversation had begun, it ended. Jeri felt the energy leave and I felt we were just getting started. I needed my answers about how to proceed.

"So does this mean I cut up the card or what?" I pleaded, not knowing the next step.

Jeri, now back to being Jeri, replied, "According to how I understood it, it's not a doing thing. It involves a shift in perception."

"And that will pay off my credit card?" I asked. I was searching for a logical solution. "I guess I could return most of it. I've kept all the receipts."

"Wouldn't you be putting out more negative energy and reinforcing your fear if you did that? Have you considered just being grateful and loving the creation, just as it is, and paying the bill as you go along?"

The truth was that I had been called on my story and my belief about fear. It would take time to digest.

Later, just as the sun was beginning to set beyond my living room window, I looked around my condo. The sun's fading hues reflected in the water casting a purple hue over a blazing red horizon. I did love this place and all the things I had purchased. I would continue to be grateful for even one hour of this magnificent view. The zone of danger was only in my thoughts. I got it: Stop spinning the story of fear. I took the card out of my wallet and kissed it. Thank you, baby! I had done it perfectly, a shining achievement made possible by MasterCard.

Some months later, my mixed creation played out in the most unusual of ways. On my way to dinner with Brian one evening, I ran out of hearing aid batteries and stopped at a store to purchase them. Just before I went into the store the battery died, but I knew I could lip-read. The salesperson was the only person at the register and when I took out my cash to pay, he asked for my address. While this was customarily done by the store for marketing purposes, he did not explain that and it made no sense to me. There was no reason to be giving out my address for a simple cash purchase. I was unsure if I actually heard the question correctly so I questioned him. Once again he repeated the request.

"I need your address," he said.

"The answer is no."

He snapped like a rubber band into an instant rage, reached across the counter, and punched me in the face, knocking off the computer monitor, which hurled me to the floor.

I ended up taking a very large company to court for the assault. I won a monetary settlement and a mandate that this company create an awareness training program for employees dealing with hearing-impaired clientele. Litigation was no trip down the yellow brick road, but in the end, I was able to pay off my total credit card debt for the furnishings and put down a down payment to buy my beautiful condo from the owner.

Even though I created a positive outcome with the settlement, in that same situation I experienced the duality of my negative creations. How was it that I would attract someone who would sense my defensiveness in not giving my address and be triggered to behave so violently?

The physical armor that I created to protect myself from hurt came from the feelings and thoughts that I had to be strong and muscular to defend myself. I feared being taken advantage of, so I often played out scenes in my mind in which I clocked someone who messed with me. The action in my thoughts attracted like action in the world of my experience. Inwardly, giving my address out to someone in a store for no reason dialed up that fear of being taken advantage of and the need to defend myself. And that energy triggered his reaction.

He said in court that he felt threatened by me because I would not answer him and so he punched me. He also had a history of three other assaults. Did it occur to him that a man buying hearing aid batteries was probably deaf?

On the positive side of the story and this creation, I had let go of the fear of not having enough money to pay my bills or buy a condo. In my mind, I acted as if I *did* own the condo and *did* have the money to pay my bills. In the absence of fear, I attracted the means to pay for both. This entire event turned out to be my own mixed creation.

Since we live in a world of duality—positive vs. negative, light vs. darkness, good vs. evil—it is no surprise that things show up as they do. We attract what we put out in our energy field. I can truly understand why we stay stuck in our own paradigm because unless something cracks us wide open with an epiphany that moves our perception out of the way, we predictably do the same things repetitively, never achieving the intended result. Instead of always asking, "What do I do?" I learned to ask, "What is it that I really want?" "How do I live from the kingdom within?"

I was about to find out.

HEARING WITHOUT EARS

chapter 15

It was a somber moment when I realized how time had marched on across my face and neck, but did it have to be on my 40th birthday? As I looked in the mirror, I began to see the early signs of aging. Thank god I was at least keeping all of my hair.

I was getting together with Jeri and her husband and a few friends to celebrate another notch on my belt. I knew I needed to stop myself from obsessing about my appearance like some of my female clients who lamented over the impending collapse of their faces, along with the addition of another chin. I had visions of my chin duplicating itself and my body adding an additional ten pounds with each decade. Had I selected a turtleneck to disguise the early stages of an emerging French crepe?

After my celebratory dinner with all its roasts and the toasts, we meandered back to the bar area for a nightcap. The loud music signified that the evening had just begun for the 11:00 p.m. bar crowd, most of them dateless and on the prowl. I was struggling to hear above the dull roar and had little interest in another DC meat market event where members of the opposite sex vied to be the selected cut of aged prime. Jeri positioned herself on a decadent leopard lounge chair that was draped in gold fringe and cushioned by red velvet pillows. Poised there, she disengaged from the lively conversation about local politics that occupied the rest of the group.

"So, Mr. Gannon, why aren't you out stalking the crowd for birthday prey?" she asked.

"Not tonight," I assured her.

"What? No birthday girl? How about at least a birthday wish?"

"I understand it is bad luck to tell," I replied.

"Well then, before the clock strikes midnight and you are no longer Cinderella, let me ask you this: If you could be or do anything you wanted by waving a magic wand, what would it be?"

"And would you be the fairy godmother?" I chuckled.

"Would I?" She quipped with one of the now famous turnaround questions.

"You mean in my career?" I asked, not quite certain where she was going with this.

"I mean anything. Don't you have a creative side you want to explore?"

"Like what?" I hedged.

"Oh, I don't know," she said.

"How about conducting an orchestra?"

"Well it might be helpful if I could hear the music first."

"It didn't stop you at the bodybuilding contest," she pointed out.

We both laughed again. Jeri had actually been the first to really collapse into hysterics when she heard the story. Everyone else had been too embarrassed for me.

"I have another good one for you," I said. "Would you believe that when I take off my hearing aid, I do hear music? I swear to it."

"Okay, so how do you know if it's really music if you can't hear what music sounds like?"

"Well, I do hear some of the tones."

"Like that racket in the next room?" she said, laughing. She was referring to the hip-hop band.

"I wonder if you hear the notes like in a melody of a song or do you hear something that sounds like music to you?"

"Wow, such deep thinking!" I fired back.

"So then you could be a conductor after all, maestro? Is that what you are telling me?"

"No, but to be truthful, I would love to sing."

"Are you serious?"

"You asked me, if I waved a magic wand and could be or do anything I want, what would it be? Now I'm telling you."

"Can you carry a tune?" she asked.

"No, not at all," I replied.

"But you want too?" she asked skeptically.

"Yes."

"So do it!" she declared.

"Have you ever heard of or known a totally deaf person who could sing?" I asked.

"No, I can't say that I have, but you once said your dream was to take on impossibility. So I say, go for it!"

"You're on!" I declared. "One day I will stand before you and these ears will sing!"

"Maybe so," she quipped, as if daring me to prove it. We toasted to the challenge and set it to rest.

It was already just seconds past midnight and, no, I had not turned into Cinderella but I needed all the fairy dust Tinkerbelle could spare to pull this singing challenge off.

It may have been the aftermath of a hangover the next day, but I started to hear myself singing on my way to see my first client. Alcohol did have its way of clouding my brain and maybe I was only hearing the pounding of my own head.

Oh wait. I remembered this was no coincidence. *Last night I promised Jeri that I would learn to sing.* It was all coming back to me in waves of clarity. My wish had been the ramblings of a drunken man on his birthday, certainly not the unleashing of a lifetime desire to sound like a seal getting kicked in the ass. I immediately dialed Jeri's number. She had to know there was no way I was ever going to burst into song like Fred Astaire. All bets were off.

"Not so fast!" Jeri said. "There you go again. Get that ego of yours out of the picture. Singing does not mean you have to be a star, or the best, or even good. Singing comes from the heart. It feels good. It puts you in touch with joy and all the things you say you want in your life. So why then does learning to sing have to turn you into someone flitting around a stage singing 'Some Enchanted Evening'?"

Her voice softened.

"Mike, don't sell out until you at least try. I saw that determination, that spark in your eye last night, and don't even dare tell me it was brought on by a few drinks or a fitful episode of diarrhea of the mouth."

Okay, this was another time when my deafness had not given me an understanding of revolting concepts like "diarrhea of the mouth." Or was it another "language by Jeri" creation? Either way, she was not letting me off the hook.

"I promise I won't give it up just yet, but don't hold your breath." That was obviously the wrong choice of words.

"What, if anything, does this have to do with my breath? This is for you! You own it, now go for it and, like I said last night, just maybe you will sing."

I said no more. She was right and I knew it. If I was going to really embrace impossibility, it needed to be more than just a few transitory thoughts about what I could accomplish.

A week or two later, I was driving in a pounding rain and dense fog. I could not see a thing in front of me, so I pulled over on the side of the road. I could barely see the shoulder but knew this spot had plenty of room for me to get completely off the road. It had been an aggravating morning that started off with oversleeping. Still unable to let go of this ridiculous notion about singing, I'd had a restless night dreaming about singing to an audience. Only no sound would come out and I kept snapping my tongue like a lizard ready to snatch an insect. Why was I in such discord over a mindless bet with Jeri? Of course I could never sing. I had certainly made that clear when I stood up for myself in grade school and got out of music class. I knew it even back then. So what did I really want? It hit me head-on.

Mike, you know what you have wanted your whole life. You might as well stop pretending. You want to hear. You want to hear! Conquering impossibility was always about hearing and you know it.

These words would not go away and repeated themselves over and over like the playground chant, "The cheese stands alone . . . the cheese stands alone."

I gripped the steering wheel and screamed, "Stop!" It was a growl of primal anger like an unleashed pit bull taunted by the confines of a rusted fence that held his rage captive.

"Why me? Why do I need to be deaf? I'm through with it! What kind of cosmic joke is this? I have nothing more to learn from being shut off from the world. God, what is it you want from me? Haven't I been through enough? I'm through with the struggle just to understand the most limited normal conversation. I hate repeating over and over again, 'What was that? Excuse me could you say that again?' I'm over staring off into space or trying to look engaged in what is being said, terrified to have others learn I had not understood a damn word of what they had just said.

"Look at me. Am I the joker with the proverbial smile? I want to be normal! Is that such a crime?" I shrieked.

"Go ahead and finish me off! Tell me what a coward I am, how there are far worse disabilities or that I am somehow special. Oh, and what about my extraordinary sense of smell? Wow that's a good quality. Or my superior eyesight so I can read lips from across the room? How about a round of applause!"

I clapped my hands, applauding myself.

My fingers stung from the force of smacking them so hard, but I was still able to make a fist so tight my fingernails gouged my skin. With my jaw clenched, I declared it over.

"I will hear. Somehow, I will hear!"

I buried my head in the steering wheel and sobbed with heaves that rattled with anguish. I raised my head and could see the visibility outside had not improved. I veered back into traffic, numb. I'd been hurt by hope before and refused to be hurt by it again. I was born profoundly deaf. The cochleae in both ears were as good as dead and short of a miracle, nothing would ever resurrect them and bring them back.

Give it up Mike. Just give it up!

めめめめめ

I loved that I could walk along the lake shoreline where I lived and in minutes arrive at the neighborhood restaurant and pub. Just as I was stepping up onto the dock, I passed a man who looked to be in his fifties. He wore what appeared to be a hearing aid behind his ear with wires going down to a device that resembled a Sony Walkman. It occurred to me that this must be a cochlear implant, a digital device that improved hearing in some deaf individuals. Neither my audiologist nor the specialist following my case had ever mentioned it to me, so I assumed it was not for my type of hearing loss. It looked like a really cumbersome contraption, so I was not entirely sure I was correct.

The next week, one of my clients Claire asked me what I thought about the heated controversy surrounding the cochlear implant. She had read an article voicing the objections of many deaf communities to this device. They felt that hearing loss should be viewed as an identity, with its own culture, rather than a disability. They strongly believed that this type of medical intervention implied the need to be fixed, rather than the acceptance of deafness as part of a wonderful subculture.

Since I had left Rochester, I had been totally removed from this world, but I was not at all surprised that some deaf people would have strong feelings about preserving the beauty of their way of communicating. However, I was perplexed that it would even be an issue. Why would anyone not wish to hear? Why would anyone wish to struggle, as I did, if there was any chance of improvement? I did have to concede that many of the deaf students I encountered had a remarkable sense of peace and serenity that I neither understood nor could claim for myself, so who was I to judge?

Claire had a very distinct and generous purpose for asking me this question.

"Mike, I know this is none of my business, but my husband and I donate to so many charities and we never see the outcome. If you're a candidate for this surgery, we would like to offer to pay for the procedure because I know the surgery and the device can cost close to $100,000."

My mouth—and my heart—dropped open. I was so totally overwhelmed by her generosity that I was speechless. Who could ever afford the procedure, even if they were eligible? I hugged her in gratitude.

"Thank you so much for thinking about me. To be honest, I don't think I'm a candidate. I'm pretty sure it's mostly used with children and that early intervention is the key."

As I spoke, the vision of the man I had seen only a week before kept flashing back into my head.

What if . . . ?

"If the day ever comes when you would consider it, will you let us know? We would love to help you," she said.

Something nagged inside of me the rest of the day. Why hadn't I at least looked into it before? Was I really that out of touch with my own disability? I called Jeri and told her about the wonderful gesture from my client. She, too, was astounded by this wonderful gesture of kindness.

"Mike," she said, "you do know I will bug you silly until you research this and at least find out more about it."

"I don't know. I really don't."

"Mike, is it that you are afraid to hear the answer?"

That was the second time that day that my mouth dropped open and I was speechless.

"Just a thought, not a question," she replied.

Maybe I was afraid of the vulnerability and the disappointment I would feel if I was not an eligible candidate and excluded from hope. Until a few weeks earlier, I had not faced what I really wanted—which was to hear. As a deaf person, I had always identified with my accomplishments. I knew I had already exceeded my expectations in many ways: academically, my speaking and lip-reading abilities, finishing college, setting up my own business, and functioning well in the hearing world. I drifted up from sleep often that night, wondering in the most deadly silence I could ever remember, who I would be without my deafness.

I had a very vivid dream just before I woke up. I was standing on a stage and I was not deaf—I never had been. I could hear perfectly and I picked up the microphone to introduce a deaf theater production. When I opened my mouth to speak about the show, no sound came out. I knew exactly what I wanted to say, but my voice was silent. One of the deaf students walked over to me after witnessing my struggle and said, "You don't have to speak, we're your voice. We feel your words from your heart."

When I woke up and reflected on this dream, I understood that there are no limitations when we let go of the boundaries that constrain us. On a conscious level, I had forgotten about my incident of having to lip sync onstage at my fourth grade concert. In my dream state, I reenacted having no voice. Unconsciously, I had held on to the experience and the resistance that went with it.

I had learned, in recent years, that struggle just created more struggle and that it fooled me into believing I was on a productive path. I had to remind myself that, according to the law of attraction, struggle carried the energy of negativity. It infected my thoughts and, not surprisingly, my patterns of behavior. I needed to let go of the pieces in my life that I felt were broken and let go of everything I carried with it from the past.

I understood that, like everyone else, I was both my best and worst judge. I remembered Jeri telling me that the only point at which eternity meets and recognizes time was in the present moment. Every moment was an opportunity to begin again.

I cancelled all my appointments for the day and began my research about the implant. By the end of the day I had an appointment for an evaluation. Jeri called mid-afternoon to ask if I had given the surgery any more thought.

"I made the appointment. Will you come with me? They have a cancellation tomorrow?"

"You are kidding me, right?"

"Absolutely not," I replied, and then paused to hear her response.

"Of course I will come . . . after you pick me up off the floor."

I did not set myself up for disappointment by anticipating the outcome. I was nervous but glad I was not going by myself. The next day, we arrived at the doctor's office and sat down to wait our turn.

"Any thoughts on which way it will go?" I asked, hoping she had some divine connection she was not sharing.

"Before you walk through that door, which I predict will be in a minute or so, make sure you can be truly happy with yourself either way, despite the outcome."

"I'm sure."

"Mr. Gannon," the nurse called, "come with me."

"Want to come in too?" I asked Jeri.

"As long as you don't tell them I'm your mother," she teased.

The doctor had already read my history and began the exam, following it with the mandatory hearing test I had taken a million times. He took a detailed medical history of my deafness and completed a very thorough examination.

He said very directly, "I'm sure you're anxious for the bottom line, so here it is. You know as we previously discussed on the phone, my answer is based on preliminary findings, but I will say, yes, I believe you are a candidate."

Thank god Jeri was there to take in the rest of what he explained because I was so elated I heard nothing past the word, "yes." *At long last, yes!* He was referring me to Johns Hopkins University Hospital.

Then it all came back to me in a flash. I had declared it so with such emotion that day on the side of the road. I had drawn it to me, from encountering the man with the implant, to my client's benevolent offer to help me finance it, to Jeri encouraging me to check it out. It was a lesson in allowing. It seemed that when I moved into a state of allowance, I allowed things to come into my life and I could accept them without judgment. I had read that we become the receivers of our creations and I was personally experiencing the truth of it.

After a few more preparatory appointments with Johns Hopkins, I was informed that I would be in and out of surgery on the same day, but that my implant wouldn't be activated until after all the swelling had gone down. That meant a thirty-day wait, during which I could only wear my left hearing aid. Talk about being really deaf! Having only my left hearing aid would make those thirty days difficult.

I also found that it was my responsibility to choose the manufacturing company I wished to use for my implant. Johns Hopkins was not at liberty to recommend which of the three companies they felt was the best. Each had its own proprietary strengths. That meant I had to do some serious research.

I finally settled on an innovative company, a subsidiary of Boston Scientific, Advanced Bionics. I felt that they were at the forefront of this technology and held the most promise for future development. The sound processor at that time was an externally belt-worn miniature computer, a pager style device with a wire that would travel up my shirt and magnetically attach to the implant inserted under my scalp. But within months after my surgery, they would convert to a behind-the-ear device, similar to a hearing aid, without the box and the cumbersome wire.

In order to place the implant surgically, it involved drilling into my skull to make an indentation for the round disk that was about the size of a fifty-cent piece. They explained they would make an incision behind the ear, pull the skin back and the ear forward, and place the implant. With great precision, a very skilled surgeon would take the noodle-like electrode attached to the implant and meticulously slip it through the cochlea of the inner ear and then close up. This electrode would stimulate the cochlea and activate the auditory nerve. So, in reality, this would be hearing without my ear.

They would only do it on one ear. The bilateral implant was still in the early stages. However, the hearing in this one ear alone would dramatically make a difference in what I could hear, in speech recognition, and the overall quality of the sound. The surgery was estimated to take approximately ninety minutes or so. Despite my jitters, I understood that this procedure had been performed on thousands of patients with very few failures. It was a go!

There was one more surprise; my health insurance covered the procedure. I thanked my client over and over again because had she not brought up the subject and offered to pay for it, I wouldn't have considered the procedure. Her generosity had birthed this possibility.

I was witnessing one thing after another falling into place, almost miraculously. When I had problems or so-called bad experiences, they were moving through me effortlessly and quickly. I only had one more thing to do before my surgery—make good on my promise to Jeri that I would sing one day.

I knew I had to find a unique kind of voice teacher because my limitations were decidedly unique. Oddly enough, I wanted to begin the experience while I still wore my hearing aids. I struggled getting past the introduction. "Hello my name is Mike and I'm profoundly deaf in both ears, but with your help, I want to learn to sing." This was like calling a dermatologist and asking him to cure an invisible rash.

I dreaded the silence and discomfort that would follow my request.

"You want to do what?"

Even in my most delusional moments, I could not imagine any reassuring reply. Maybe I could phrase it differently and say, "I would like to explore an alternative method of vocalizing that would enable me to match pitch and tone to a melody while excluding hearing." That might at least divert the focus.

I sat in quiet contemplation for a few moments waiting for the courage to even make the phone call. I returned to that early time in my life when the most angelic and beautiful music had filled my heart. However, this time I not only heard it, I was part of the performance. I felt the swell in my chest as I brought in enough breath to expand my lungs and then push through my vocal chords, into my throat, and out of my mouth. I was singing! I was not trapped onstage as an insecure and frightened little boy, dubbing in words masqueraded as music and hiding behind garish looking hearing aids too large for my head. I needed no road map for this journey; I had already begun with the end in mind. I hired a well-trained voice teacher on the faculty at Catholic University, one who had come personally recommended by one of my father's coworkers.

Laurie was also a highly accomplished opera singer and did private lessons for her students, preparing them for higher study and training. So I was not exactly her typical client. I explained my fears and my limitations, and what I wished to accomplish. She did not so much as blink an eye. I loved her for that. The slightest hesitation might have made me bolt out the door. We connected immediately and her graciousness put me at ease.

We started with a simple five-note scale. My memory of trying to fit into my fourth grade music class returned. I could not vocalize a single note, but it did not deter her in the least. We kept right on going with my crooning and croaks, as if I were among her best students. We started working on tongue placement by mimicking the word "anga," which sounded weird, especially when we had to make it as nasal as possible. I made such contorted faces that we both burst into laughter. It was a perfect match of personality and endurance.

This time I was determined to sing, or at least not hide behind the sound that I made. It did not matter that I was off pitch, which was frequent, or that the person who had a lesson after me was a student preparing to try out for a position at Juilliard. That student must have either felt like a star or wore earplugs in the waiting room.

I continued to work and be inspired by Laurie, who sang like an angel and acted as if I did the same. It was such a liberating feeling to be able to connect to my heart and belt out the words. I loved it, no matter how I sounded. I kept up my daily vocal exercises, for the sheer joy of sound. I knew my pitch and ability to carry a tune would improve after the implant, but I didn't care.

I appreciated the study of music in all its forms. I bought a keyboard and a set of drums. I wore out my copy of *Music for Dummies*. I discovered that Laurie's fiancé Brad taught drumming and knew that there was no better way for me to learn to follow the beat than through a rhythmic vibration. Drumming became my ego booster. My hand-eye coordination had paid off.

The great novelist Victor Hugo once said, "Music expresses that which cannot be put into words and cannot remain silent." I understood that completely.

I was soon to become a bionic man, but in truth, that bionic man was being created on the inside, from that place of connection to a higher source. I would embrace impossibility and I would hear.

I learned that visualization within the mind is what gives our conscious energy form, and it is our heart that gives that form life. My head and my heart were aligned. Someday these ears would sing!

THE HOOKUP

chapter 16

Mind plus heart produces results. I knew it. I had lived it. And yet, the day of my surgery, my hands shook more than my electric toothbrush. It seemed that visualizing something happening in the future was quite different than stepping into it on any given day.

Tom, a college friend, and Jeri agreed to lend moral support for my big day. I knew that the two of them would ease my nerves with a comedy routine that would distract me from going under the knife. They were true to form and we laughed the entire way to Johns Hopkins through the typical Washington/Baltimore extreme rush hour. It was the predictable hospital plan: hurry up, get there early, and then wait. My anxiety was building as the hour hand was approaching one o'clock.

The surgical waiting room was packed and for the very first time, I was thankful I could not eat. The disinfectant smell alone was enough to churn any gastric remains into liquid groceries and hurl them across the waiting room. Jeri was fascinated by the medical surroundings and created a clinical guessing game around why each person needed surgery. Tom was actually turning approximately the same shade of green as me, so when the nurse apprehended me for the preoperative ordeal, I was relieved rather than anxious. I was outfitted with the typical rear end tie-up robe that exposed my glaringly white gluteus maximus to the max. I clasped it from behind and held on as tightly as an old lady clutching her handbag.

The surgical attendants were all very cheerful as they executed the preoperative mandates in preparation for the final intravenous drip that would whisk me away into pharmaceutical never-never land. I could feel myself drifting off, oblivious to the fact that I might have mooned some of Johns Hopkins' patients. A few of the residents scrubbing in for my surgery stopped by to introduce themselves and ask if I had any other questions. I was too oblivious to respond.

I must have dozed off a bit before they took me to the surgical suite and loaded me on the table to await my implantation. It seemed I had already signed multiple informed release documents proclaiming every doom and gloom scenario when "Nurse Ratchet" walked in with yet another pronouncement. Her voice faded in and out as she officiously reminded me that when I woke up, I could feel dizzy or nauseous, I could vomit, and that the implant could fail—which would mean that I could not even return to my hearing aid because the insertion of the electrode destroys the cochlea totally in order for the new signal to take over. She also discussed the possibility of facial paralysis and a host of other monstrous side effects, including but not limited to death.

I felt disconnected from my body and my thoughts. I was about to yield to the anesthesia, just as Mattie had done before he surrendered on the surgical table and never returned home. A very kind nurse named Joanne, whom I had met during my presurgery visits, took my hand. I held her hand tightly and realized that I did not have any control over what was going to happen in the next two hours. I looked into Joanne's eyes and made an amazing connection to her heart. I felt as if I were looking into the eyes of Spirit when she smiled. Tears of gratitude welled up in my eyes and that was the last thing I would later remember happening before the operation.

I awoke in the recovery room with an earmuff on my head that resembled a baseball, howling that my butt hurt! Apparently they had rolled me over during surgery and injected me with a painkilling solution via a mile long needle. It felt like someone had jabbed me with a pitchfork. Tom was the first person I recognized standing over my bed. He looked no better than when I had left him that morning. He did not have the stomach for this. Jeri was off to my left talking to the nurse as if she could run the postoperative suite herself. Apparently they were not going to let me return home that night and she was sorting out the details.

I felt an uncontrollable nausea rumble in like a roller coaster heaving my body into retching convulsions. Tom ran for cover and all that came up from my huge, diaphragmatic thunder was a little bit of spit. However, it had sealed the deal; I was on my way in a gurney across the entire complex through a tunnel to my overnight stay. Since there were no beds available on any of the surgical floors, I was laid to rest in the heart transplant unit.

There was just one problem: the pain medication had erased my ability to recall being in the recovery room and I woke up hours later surrounded by all the bells and whistles of life support on an organ transplant floor. What had happened to the in-and-out surgery scenario? It was in the middle of the night and Jeri and Tom had already left. Someone had put a sign that said "deaf patient" on my door. As a result, no nurse who came in to attend to me spoke to me. Thank god for the morphine!

Jeri and Brian arrived early the following morning to bring me home. I was touched to see my brother there too. I had not even thought of including him in my arrangements, but he was there for me and that was all that mattered.

For the next few days, I realized my balance was totally out of alignment. I had to be careful not to stand up too quickly or I would be dizzy. As a hypnotherapist, it crossed my mind that the final, negative suggestions administered under the auspices of informed consent might have affected my postoperative recovery—particularly since they had been given while I was under a drug-induced receptive state. It was entirely possible that these fear-based thoughts, just prior to my final dose of anesthesia, had adversely affected my body-mind connection. The power of suggestion in a heightened state of fear just prior to a drug induced loss of consciousness might not have been such an enlightened decision, even if it was Johns Hopkins, arguably the best hospital in the country.

But I was regaining more of my stamina with each day and the incision was healing quite nicely. Jeri chided me about my shaved head and my dazed state and insisted that I could have auditioned for a punk version of *The Rain Man*. I could feel at times that I was shuffling rather than walking to maintain my balance. And for the first week or so, I had a hard time focusing on a conversation. It was like someone had pushed a button marked "brainless" and I was stuck in that mode. My condo smelled like a funeral home with all the flowers from friends and clients, but it was still a great feeling to have such support and thoughtful reminders of their affection for me.

Waiting to know if the surgery had worked was torture. After all, someone had to comprise the one percent failure rate. Why was it taking me longer to heal when most reported being up and running in a day or so? I was a health conscious, physically fit person and ideal surgical candidate, so what was the problem? Realistically, I knew that most of the implanted populations were children with rebound abilities superior to those of an adult. In the interim, I would lie in bed at night and visualize the activation as successful. One particular night, I was not as restless as usual and something from within told me to pick up my pen and write. I was told not to go to my computer, but just to go to my heart and allow the words to come.

What words?

"Just write, Mike, just write."

Write what?

"You will know."

And so I did. That night, in a semi-lit room and at a time when most people were already asleep, I wrote what could have been lyrics to a song. But there was a message embedded within.

To Mattie:

The Child Who Dances in My Eyes

Mom, I do not hear your voice, but your
arms are all I need,

For you to hold me next to your breast
when it is time to feed.

It's not your fault; you cannot know that
my world is very still,

No one told you that I am deaf and I don't
know when they will.

Just hold me tight, next to your heart, and
I will feel so safe,

I will use my eyes to smile at you and
touch your loving face.

They gave you the news, I could not hear
soon after I was two,

And already the miracle of another son
grew inside of you.

Did you make him just for me? Is he to be
my ears?

Can he take away the silence and ease
away my fears?

I held him close when you brought him
home. I rocked him on my knee

And I would love my little brother that
God had sent to me.

His fingers and toes were moving fast, no
noise that I could hear,

But a musical rhythm I felt so soft and
sweetly clear.

I was just a little boy back then, but as a
man it is no surprise,

Matt had come to be the child who dances
in my eyes.

We played together every day. He was the
best friend I would know

Until God came to take him home to a
place I could not go.

I remember he was pale and thin and
Mom called him frail,

But he never let us notice that his heart
began to fail.

You brought him to the hospital; he left
with an angel one day,

And in that single moment, the dance had
gone away.

There was no more music in my life, no
dance that I could see,

Only my little brother, who had meant the
world to me.

Many years passed me by, until an
implant replaced my ear

And Matt's spirit danced in my eyes, as he
whispered,

"You can hear."

I knew beyond all doubt that the surgery was successful. Mattie had never left and he would be the first to tell me that it was a go!

My mom came up to be present for the implant activation. She was the one who first knew that I was deaf. It was only fitting that she be at my side when I first heard in a range that had historically been impossible. Jeri joined us as well. She too had been such an intricate part of this whole process and without her undaunting encouragement, I might have never claimed this moment. I was still having bouts of vertigo, which was not conducive to navigating in rush hour traffic, so Jeri assumed the chauffeur role as well.

We arrived and were escorted to a colorful waiting room where a three-year-old child also awaited treatment. I noticed she wore a cochlear implant and spoke perfectly as she pretended to read a book out loud to her mother. No one would have known she was hearing-impaired, had it not been for the implant she wore. I could not help but wonder how my life would have been different—and how much less struggle I might have endured—had this technology been available to me from the onset. I was fascinated watching the child interact with such assuredness, as if she had no care in the world. I wondered what my mom was thinking. How much easier her life would have been, had Tracy and I heard. She'd had to fight for the minimal special education programs available to us at the time while also keeping us connected to the hearing world. I glanced over to see if she was watching this diminutive person, but she seemed detached and stared straight ahead. I knew better than to ask how she felt because her answer would have been, "Oh honey, it was just fine with all of you children." Not that I ever expected her to say, "Yeah, your handicap was a real downer," but I craved honest emotions from her and the smile that had once made my whole world safe.

I remembered a night before Mattie's last surgery, after she had put us all to bed. When she looked down at me, snuggled in my bed, I had felt the most amazing connection of love. It was an unspoken moment that I had not recalled in a very long time. Mom was still a very nice looking woman, despite her advancing years. People always liked her, but how many really knew her? And after all the years of living alone, did she even really know herself?

The moment had come for me to embrace my Star Trek persona. My "hookup" resembled a sci-fi transmitter, but even if it was a hat with flowers growing out of my head, I was ready to embrace it at this point. We all filed into a small, very sterile room and huddled around the monitor. We were transfixed, waiting to witness the electrodes give birth to sound. I was introduced to my new audiologist, Dawn, who I liked immediately. She could tell I was nervous and made every effort to explain each move executed on her computer.

This was just the beginning of my journey into digitally fine-tuning my world. I knew not to expect clear sounds right away. It would take several mappings before I would witness any progress. I was ready. Mom was stoic and Jeri appeared to be suppressing a grin, as if something was funny.

Ready . . . set . . . launch. Dawn was rapping her knuckles under the desk and asked if I could identify the sound. The program was sending signals up to approximately 30,000 pulses per second, a significant difference from the input I was accustomed to receiving with my hearing aid. I felt the vibration more than the sound itself, all the way to my toes. The best way I could describe it was like a blaring radio, improperly tuned, buzzing in my ear. Dawn reassured me that it could take the brain some time to adjust before things started to sound natural again. Even though I knew not to expect instant sound recognition, somewhere imbedded in my imagination, I expected the "Halleluiah Chorus" to fill the air, when actually everyone sounded more like Mickey Mouse! She made a few more adjustments and with the assurance it would be much clearer in a few days, I was out the door. Oh my god, what had I done? Thank god I had perfected the art of lipreading.

It was lunchtime and Jeri insisted on a celebration, knowing I would be obsessing about sound unless I had my mind occupied elsewhere. What better place than the Baltimore Harbor, bustling with lunchtime activity. Street vendors and outdoor restaurants proved to be a welcome diversion. Everything sounded like a digital buzz and that was the biggest hurdle that kept me from hearing clearly. The rest would be about adaptation and fine-tuning over time. When Mom excused herself to visit the ladies room, I was dying to find out from Jeri what she had found so amusing just prior to my activation.

"Oh that," she giggled. "Well, it was certainly evident that the staff is more adept at dealing with children. I suppose you didn't hear your sweet audiologist ask, 'Are you ready for me to turn you on?' Hardly appropriate terminology for an adult male, wouldn't you say?"

We both were laughing as my mother returned wanting to know what was so amusing. Jeri covered up quickly recalling a hysterical anecdote that she pulled out of nowhere and entertained my mother without skipping a beat. She had known that Mom would have gone into outright cardiac arrest with such a lewd insinuation at this very special moment in my life. I found myself hoping to someday acquire Jeri's mastery of social correctness.

We left the city in a silhouette of fading sun signaling the end of day. I wondered how I would manage the digital input without resistance. Somewhere in my reading I had learned that the brain adapts faster when you positively welcome the input of new sound. I sat down that night, secluded in my room, and the memory of that very first day I went with my father for my hearing aids returned. My mind drifted as the words fell in place. I was hearing the voice of my father talking to me, reassuring me that I need not be afraid. It had been a long time since I had revisited that place of warm security. I wrote the following words as if I were in that moment.

Can You Hear the Leaves Blowing in the Wind?

*My father gazed out the window. An hour
had gone by.*

*In the interim of that silence, he breathed
a heavy sigh.*

*Was he only watching as the leaves fell to
the ground?*

*Did he hear the wind that roared a strong
and gusty sound?*

*Dad had a certain knowing that came in
later years,*

*A heart filled with emotion that would fill
his eyes with tears.*

*"Son," he said to me, "have I told you
about that day?*

243

They told us you were deaf; there were no words you could say.

"To think there was no sound, deaf in both your ears,

You never heard our voice to soothe away your fears.

"The day you got your hearing aids, I carried you out the door,

The leaves were blowing everywhere, the wind began to soar.

"I looked upon your tiny face, your eyes so very blue,

I knew you heard the wind although it frightened you.

"As I reached down for a leaf and held it to your head,

You knew the leaf could talk, no matter what I said.

"Let that be a lesson when the season comes around,

The leaf that's fallen on the ground is more than just a sound.

"It is never in the present time that we learn what love can hold,

It is later in the memories that truth is fonder told.

*"So when I get to heaven and make a
brand new start,
Always know the leaves that blow are
footprints on my heart.*

*"And when the wind is blowing, know that
I am near,
Remember the crunching leaves that said,
'My little boy can hear!'"*

I had no idea that the months ahead of me would be so
enriched by the newness and discovery of the hearing world—
starting with crickets! I could remember hearing what I believed to
be crickets as a child, but as I grew into adulthood, that sound had
faded. I was stunned at the myriad of sounds and pitches emitted
in unison by these small little creatures. Mostly when I walked my
dog, I could recognize different pitch and the orchestration of an
entire insect population that I could not even see.

Also, for the very first time, I could hear birds chirping
outside my bedroom window. I was surprised that they had such
clearly distinctive chirps. And even more incredible was my ability to
discern their fast talk as each morning dawned with new conversation.
I had always heard my neighbors complain about the noisy Canadian
geese that inhabited the lake. I was astounded by the ruckus they
created as nature sounded its new presence in my life.

I was constantly challenged with identifying and making
out sounds that I had never heard before. I discovered with great
glee that my cereal did indeed snap, crackle and pop! I was like a
five-year-old each time I poured the milk, putting my ear close

to the bowl and taking delight in the fact that it would always perform its number. I noticed small things that most people take for granted, such as the disharmony of the refrigerator motor with the buzz of the dishwasher, surrounded by the background hum of the air conditioning unit. These were often distractions to me, especially when I lapsed into noise overload.

However, I was determined to embrace all sounds as a gift, knowing my resistance might delay the adaptation process. I knew that the faster the identification I make of any sound positively imprinted on my brain, the easier it would become. I was also fascinated when people said they did not even know these background sounds were in the room. I was not quite ready for the lesson on selective hearing. I had already been too long on the other side of the fence.

I went back to Johns Hopkins for mapping every three months for the first year. This is when they hooked up the processor I wore on my belt to their computer. They tested for the most comfortable loudness and the softest sounds that I could hear. The difference between the two spreads was called the dynamic range, or what I was capable of hearing. This determined the decibel level of hearing as well as the megahertz from the lowest pitch to the highest.

As my brain adapted to the new input from the processor, my dynamic range increased over time. By the end of my first three-month period, I was hearing more things than ever before. I could hear my breathing. I could hear my shoes scraping against the surface beneath me. I could hear my fingernails scratch the surface of my skin. Life was sounding more alive with each new day, connecting me with a deeper emotion that resonated with every aspect of my life.

My progress was tremendous. My only problem was the digital aspect still kicked in from time to time making word recognition seem even harder. In the beginning, the outside world of sound came in digitally because the brain had not adapted to the frequency. It took the first year to map the computer-based program in such a way to eliminate this interference. The initial digital input was fading as my brain was adapting and converting the signals into recognizable, auditory sounds. But the technology was very sophisticated and it took time for my brain and the programmed frequencies to sync up. I tried not to rely on my lipreading skills, but after so many years, it was difficult to forego my backup strategy. Dawn switched me to different programs that opened a whole new world of clarity. Everything sounded so much more natural.

The one downside was that I was able to hear my own voice. Everyone had always remarked at what excellent speaking skills I had acquired from my early years of speech therapy. You could have fooled me. To me, it sounded like I had cotton balls stuffed up my nose when I spoke. I remembered what my singing teacher had taught me about using my diaphragm. I knew I was ready to return to my vocal lessons with Laurie. Even if I could not sing right away, I could still improve my speaking ability by working with the tonality of my voice.

Another surprise was bathroom noise! I never would have believed that in relieving myself, I sounded like a hydrant hose responding to a three-alarm fire. I had no idea that every "plop" in the toilet bowl or that the passing of gas had its own recognizable sound.

I was just on the breaking edge of technology and I became one of the first users of the behind-the-ear device that replaced the belt-worn processor. What a relief to go wireless. It looked much like my old hearing aid, with the only difference being a wire extending from my behind-the-ear processor to the same electrode disk that connected to the surgically buried implant.

I hadn't realized just how much my life had truly changed until one cool spring morning. I was preparing my boat—known as "the party barge"—for a barbeque with friends. It had not yet been cleaned from the winter months, so I had a few hours of work ahead of me. As I leaned over to pick up something from the side of the boat, I momentarily lost my balance. As I was coming back up, the back of my right ear grazed the cross ropes that supported the canopy. In that split second, my behind-the-ear device flipped into the air and disappeared into the murky lake.

I froze. It was impossible to determine or see where it had landed. All that was visible was the despondent reflection of my own face reflecting back to me the horrible truth: It was gone!

I telephoned Jeri, forgetting for a moment that I could not hear. In that daunting moment of stone deafness, I realized how much I depended on this new connection to my world. I decided to call her anyway and assumed she would pick up and, at the very least, hear what I had to say. I could not hear the phone ringing on her end, so I decided to wait ten to fifteen seconds before I started speaking.

"Jeri! I don't know if you're on the line right now, but I am going to assume you can hear me. I can't hear you because my BTE fell into the lake! If you're there, I need your help. It won't do you any good to speak back to me, but just stay where you are and I'll be at your house in a few minutes! I need you to call Advance Bionics for me."

I raced over to Jeri's place to see if she was home. She was not. I was really feeling helpless at this point and I decided to sit in the car and wait for her to return. She arrived approximately thirty minutes later.

The bad news got worse when she made the call. My piece was covered by insurance for damage, but not for loss. I had not understood that part when purchasing the insurance and the device itself was close to $7,500 to replace. Jeri was told I needed the actual device in my possession in order to collect the damages and replace it. There was no way I was going to find it and it would most certainly be damaged because it had already been in the lake for about forty-five minutes. The water around the boat was eight to ten feet deep, with an undercurrent that was particularly strong.

I decided that despite the odds, I had no choice but to go back to the dock and go diving for it. One of my neighbors graciously offered to help with the search, even though we collectively agreed I needed a miracle. As I stood on the barge next to mine looking into the water, I took a moment to silence my fearful mind chatter and reconnect with my place of divine stillness. I silently prayed. *My beloved God, I am going to begin with the end in mind. Thank you for this miracle and for returning my implant to me.*

I created a feeling of absolute certainty, opened my eyes, and dove into the lake fully clothed, shoes and all. I came up to the surface and asked Jeri to take the collapsible pole I had stored on the boat and hold it in the approximate area where I had last seen my BTE enter the lake. Once that was set, I took a moment to catch my breath and dove to the bottom. I could barely see the aluminum pole. Everything around me was cloaked in darkness. In a moment I call magical, a ray of sunlight pierced the water from above and illuminated a nearby rock. I still couldn't see well, but I noticed a blob on top of it. I reached out and scooped up what I instantly recognized as my BTE!

I came up to the surface, cleared my eyes, and looked at Jeri, beaming a smile across my face. I held the BTE triumphantly in the air as if waving a flag of victory. Everyone who had gathered by the dock cheered along with me. I looked towards the heavens to follow the only sunlight that had pierced the overcast sky. A small opening in the clouds had allowed the sun to show me where my device had fallen. As I looked at it, the light faded away behind the gray cloud from which it had emerged. The God of my silence had once more answered my prayer.

Jeri called the same customer service representative at Advance Bionics to tell her my news. She was speechless but happy that they would be able to replace the device within twenty-four hours. But the unexplained miracles were not over. I decided to see just how waterlogged it had become. I turned it on. After being in the lake for more than an hour, it worked perfectly. This was impossible! Even the slightest residue of moisture could throw it off and permanently damage the unit.

Once again it confirmed for me that when we consciously use our thoughts to attract our desired experiences, we cocreate with a higher power. On this day, I was "hooked up" to more than sound; I was hooked up to the "big guy" himself.

෩෩෩෩෩

The months that followed were the greatest hearing experiences of my life. I often reflect back on that overwhelming experience of new sound. Today I go through life doing the things I have already experienced millions of times, but I have the instant understanding and appreciation of the miracle of hearing.

I learned that intense passion is born in the soul with our spirit taking the lead. Our job is to follow through when the opportunity arises and trust that our thoughts and feelings will become powerful creators. Doubts often perpetuated by our rational thought processes tell us we are not enough to fulfill our dreams. Struggle and resistance impedes that higher vibration and slows down the process. I learned that the root of passion is the joy found in the present moment.

I can now hold conversations with people walking or sitting behind me. I can make out the commentator's voice on the radio, and I enjoy audiobooks in my car. My younger sister, Tracy, also followed in my footsteps and underwent this surgery with remarkable success. We actually communicated for the first time on the telephone without exasperation. Can I hear an ant walk? Well, maybe not.

The cochlear implant technology is one of the greatest successes of modern medicine and has invited the deaf community to partake of a world made rich by sound. Yet, it is only one aspect of the vast abilities gifted to us as humans. So long as we hold the belief that our thoughts create our reality, all things are possible. The flicker of every thought held in the imagination does far more than offer us opportunities to grow. It is the divine gift of choice and the self-made blueprint that create the very hookups of our tomorrows.

THE LAW OF ATTRACTION IN ACTION

chapter 17

The process of normalizing the sound from my implant was a changing event with each mapping. I refused to buy into the statistic that children tended to have better results than adult recipients. I listened to music nonstop and could feel myself steadily improving. Luckily, every three months I had mappings and hearing tests with word recognition scores to monitor my conversational progress. I closed my eyes and listened to the television so I could practice hearing without reading lips. My belief that I could hear perfectly remained a constant, even through minor adjustment issues.

I stopped thinking of myself as a hearing-impaired person. I felt so much more confident communicating and I took the time to offer gratitude for every new sound, every successful telephone conversation, and every time I functioned well in a group with background noise. Nothing could hold me back. I was prepared to make quantum leaps in my growth. I chose only the highest thoughts about my improvement and considered any bump in the road an opportunity to expand. Using and understanding the law of attraction, I became a magnet for the highest possible options to exceed my goals. I had intuitively used these principles for most of my life, so I was already on the inside track of knowing it worked.

I became active in a volunteer mentoring program to assist other potential implant recipients. I spoke at one of the National Advanced Bionics Conferences in Atlanta to parents considering implants for their profoundly deaf children. I told them my life story and spoke from my heart about the difficulty with hearing aids and my frustration functioning in the hearing world. I stressed to them that I never gave up the belief that one day I could and would live surrounded by the richness of sound. I could see in their faces the anxious, desperate worry of having a child unable to function in ways that other children took for granted. A young mother came up to me after my speech.

"Tonight I will sleep reassured for the first time since I found out my eighteen-month-old little girl was diagnosed as profoundly deaf. I have been so overwhelmed with making this decision to implant her. It took courage to tell your story. I needed to hear every word you said. I felt your pain and what you went through and the courage it took to share. As afraid as I am for her, I want to give her every chance to be like other kids. Thank you so much for being here and paving the way."

I hugged her and she promised to let me know how she was doing after the surgery. I knew right then, this was the living law of attraction in action. We will attract what we need, in an abundant universe that gives us choice.

I had some rethinking to do for myself. I had already chosen a career working with people's bodies to get them in shape and although I still loved this field, I became more conscious of holistically integrating physical and spiritual well-being into my program. I loved to see the results my clients experienced, the smiles on their faces, and the resurrected self-confidence it allowed. I would also be able to expand my ability to generate more income. Once Jeri and I attended the class about attracting wealth and abundance, my switch stayed in the "on" position.

I was consistently in tune with how my emotions and thoughts influenced every aspect of my being. I learned the importance of constantly checking in with how I felt about what I wished to change or create. I was determined to teach people how to use their minds to create what they wanted. Early on, I learned from my workouts how to connect kinesthetically with my own body and dramatically increase my strength and capabilities. I pursued any type of learning that fostered the importance of the body-mind connection.

Jeri and I were avid proponents of Neuro-linguistic Programming (NLP), which deals with human behavior on the level of neurology, language, and programming. Although the training itself is primarily a cognitive process of self-discovery, it models the untapped vision and unlimited potential of communication. Jeri learned of a comprehensive NLP certification program that could be completed in nine months. The training was fascinating and we received our certification as NLP practitioners. School had been such a great effort for me, but now it was the one thing that set me on fire. I finally had the language, the skills, and the arena in which to put it all together.

With growing confidence, I began offering corporate wellness programs. Smaller fitness facilities began to emerge in office buildings to encourage better health and practices to reduce stress among employees. I offered group training that incorporated nutrition, diet, and lifestyle, as well as exercise. It became a wild success. Within six months, I had transformed my schedule from one that relied exclusively on personal training to a more balanced combination that produced results. I was hand selected by the CEO of Vance International, one of the largest executive protection security companies in the world, to head up their fitness and wellness program.

Especially after my NLP training, I was able to devise programs that enriched a person's map of success and ability to make choices based on a different understanding of perception. I incorporated visualization, meditation, and self-hypnosis techniques to repattern unwanted behavior. My substantial increase in income provided renewed inspiration towards my bigger dreams.

As a trainer, I have heard every excuse in the world about diet: too much, too little, too late. I was also well aware of the effects of negative thinking on the body that remained in a person's energy field. When it comes to our physicality, this is an area where we, collectively and habitually as a society, abuse, degrade, despise, poison, and disrespect our bodies. If we included these acts in the criminal code as vagrant and depraved behavior with wanton disregard for human life, how many would be guilty of these atrocities? We are enthralled by the Hollywood image of the beautiful body and we will dangerously starve ourselves, take illegal drugs, emulate, glorify, and set our standards for who we love and accept solely based on how they look.

I shifted my approach from what clients told me about their diet habits to how they felt about themselves. When it came to what they thought and felt, I understood that they would attract it and become it. I needed to teach that. I observed a real desperation around food, what to eat, when to eat it, how much, the number on the scale, or the size they wore. I decided to try an experiment in which I would casually hand them a piece of paper and tell them I was going to name a body part and they were to write down the first thing that came to their mind. Most of my clients in this group were women, but what transpired absolutely amazed me. I would go in random order and throw out the names of different body parts—arms, neck, shoulders, chest, back, abdomen, buttocks, thighs, and calves—and ask them to write down the first thing that came into their minds. Out of about thirty subjects, most wrote judgments about size: too big, too fat, too lumpy, too flabby, my worst feature, embarrassing, jiggling, pathetic—every negative thing you could imagine. Occasionally, they would say they liked a particular feature over the others. The most amazing thing to me was that not one of them ever mentioned how they were blessed with the function of that body part. No one said their thighs supported their body or that their legs allowed them to walk, or that their arms let them hug or hold their child or gave them the ability to carry groceries. Functionality took an overwhelming defeat over appearance. If it was too big a leap for them to begin loving how their body looked, they could at least learn to be grateful for what it allowed them to do. Jeri, who was a lifetime veteran of dieting, applied these concepts to her body image with great success. Together we started group seminars, which focused on these principles.

We explained to our clients how their judgments about food created a mental filter, that it is a mental model we construct to contain all our thoughts, feelings, and knowledge. We suggested that they imagine it covered by a grid, such as a fencing mask, that kept out certain types of awareness and that people use this as protection to keep them from facing the unfavorable notions they hold about their bodies. In breaking down old patterns, the grid did not need to be changed. Rather, the entire structure needed to be dismantled, allowing the person to let go of all the old stuff inside that governed their world. If the old stuff was left in place, lasting change didn't happen. Only superficial issues would be addressed. Like the law of attraction, the key was to gently but firmly allow that structure to dismantle and be replaced by more encouraging thoughts and feelings.

We did the same with food, instructing clients to eat only when they were hungry and with one caveat: to eat only what they loved. That worked better than any food plan they had tried. I asked them to stop thinking about what would make them fat, because the very thought about the food was as fattening as the food itself. What you think, becomes. This is one of the cornerstones of the law of attraction. The only rule was to eat when they were hungry and stop immediately when they were full, with emphasis on absolutely loving everything they put into their body.

We discussed the bombardment of judgment we put on what we eat, such as, "that makes me fat," or "this has too many calories," or even "this is delicious but fattening." These are all negative judgments we hold about the food we eat. I asked them to think about how much negative energy and resistance was held within those thoughts. I pointed out that whenever someone says she doesn't like something about her body, she creates a place of nonacceptance within herself. Likewise, if a person blocks off hurt, that person blocks the ability to feel. And to judge another based on some societal set of standards separates the person judging from the ability to love—and be loved—unconditionally. All these separations cumulatively add up to taking us further away from the source that renders us whole and divine. I wanted to help restructure a healthy body image so they did not have to feel compelled to look a certain way.

Our bodies process foods differently when we place a negative judgment on the food: "This is bad." "This is diet food." "This isn't enough." But if we loved what we ate, our bodies would process the food much more healthily. It was amazing to me how we unconsciously programmed our minds to store our food as the pounds we believe they represent. I also determined the extent to which food was the only comfort in a client's life, which made it a substitute for socializing instead of a source of nutrition. I felt that addiction of any kind was fed by thought and emotion and there was never enough of the addictive substance to fill the void. Rather than continuing to adhere to strict fitness guidelines, I, too, changed my own perspective and understanding. Each person had their own set of circumstances that needed to be revisited. What they thought to be true manifested in pounds.

I learned that being overweight was often a symptom of the problem of "feeling lack," a problem that wore many faces. I saw the gut-wrenching pain that accompanied my clients' obesity and I also saw the intensity of their quest to feel attractive, which they believed would accompany weight loss. There was an implied assumption that being thin would bring love and admiration. I wondered who we had become when poundage determined who was loved and admired. How cruelly we treat each other in the name of appearance and how unenlightened we are to believe that body size and shape represent more than a smidgeon of who we are in eternal terms.

When I made a decision to do something and felt it from my heart, I knew that unknown forces were already at work bringing it into being. Jeri and I both enrolled in spiritual healing classes, which later led us to become Reiki and Healing Touch practitioners. Energy fields are interwoven like a sweater into the fabric of our aliveness. Our training helped others to restore health and balance in their lives. We still retain the clients that have been with us since the beginning. We have experienced miraculous results in doing adjunctive therapy with cancer patients. I have devised a program that teaches stroke victims how to visualize moving their arms and legs and it has met with great success. I pulled from my own experience of how my brain learned to adapt to the digital signals from my cochlear implants. Focused visualization and intent, followed by consistent application, helped my stroke clients develop new neurological pathways. The process helped expedite the functionality of their extremities. In fact, all of the cases I worked with shortened the anticipated length of physical therapy by almost half. It was another example of how the visualizing and believing produced consistent results utilizing the law of attraction.

Jeri was also successful using the law of attraction in combination with her use of Reiki, hypnosis, guided meditation, and spiritual counseling to assist clients suffering from anxiety disorders and depression. The common denominator in all these modalities is that they embolden the universal truth that we are self-creators—

we each hold within ourselves the ultimate choice of who we are and who we are willing to become.

Jeri and I decided that we needed to reach more people in different walks of life and completed a certification program as Life/Success Coaches. We also wanted to teach the law of attraction and coach others to manifest their destiny. The school where we received our training was an absolute gift right before our eyes, a very well established, spiritually based life coaching accreditation program called SUN, which stands for Success Unlimited Network.

Interestingly, the founder of SUN lived directly across the lake from my home. From the first time I set eyes on the lake where I had visualized my condo, I felt the energy of new life. We had been sharing the same setting sun over the lake for a long time before we met. And now another SUN had taken on significance in my life. It gave me the direction and skills to really listen and put my voice aside so that I could empower others to hear *their* own voices.

Together Jeri and I formed a partnership within the Success Unlimited Network umbrella. Our approach is a disciplined focus on attracting your best life. Many seek direction to determine their own life purpose and how to go about living it from day to day. We maintain that we are not problem solvers, we are more like a moving company to support others in relocating from where they are in life to where they wish to be. We find that clients remain stuck when they are unable to determine their life purpose or release the destructive thinking patterns that keep them from reaching their goals.

We were also fortunate with our timing. Although literature, religious traditions, and philosophies have alluded to the law of attraction for centuries, it has once again gained more recognition in the last decade. Ester and Jerry Hicks, who we have deeply admired over the years, have published volumes of writings on the universal law of attraction channeled from a collective group consciousness. The best selling publication *The Secret* by Rhonda Byrne burst onto the public scene with immense acknowledgement. Her contemporary and practical application of the law of attraction made it user friendly and has influenced others to help disseminate related information and approaches. We have been blessed with many contributors to this great lesson in self-creation.

I know—even from childhood experiences—that when I have been able to identify what I wanted, when I felt how it would feel, and when I saw it with clear vision, I attracted the means I needed to bring it into my life. However, the magical thinking that "we can have anything we want" is only one of the beliefs. One problem still remains. Our thinking processes are often infiltrated with things like: success only comes to the rich; I must work hard to get ahead; I don't deserve to have what I want, or; I'm not smart enough. In my case, that limiting belief was that success would elude me because I was deaf. A lifetime of limiting beliefs and feelings do not disappear because we read in a book that we can attract a shiny new red Mercedes. When we do not get what we want, we feel that the law of attraction is just another money making scam and false promise. But look what will also happen. We will attract more evidence to support that conclusion. Like attracts like. We will set in motion all the things to come to us that will show how we are absolutely right. And when that dream Mercedes passes us on the street and is driven by someone else, it is because that is exactly what we are giving our attention to: more wanting and other people having.

Both Jeri and I discovered that clients sought out the law of attraction mostly in the area of relationships, wealth, and fulfillment. Since joy is usually the underlying emotion we seek, we would ask clients to name a few things that made them feel happy. Typically, clients had an easier time determining what made them unhappy. Often the problem showed up for them as circumstances outside of themselves such as issues with their jobs, money, the kids, their spouse, or any other aspect of life. This is what they had put their attention on, and this is what they have received—more of the same. Then the question becomes, "Since I have no control over how 'they' are acting, and it affects me, how do I change these circumstances and get what I want?"

The answer is to focus on what you do want and how it makes you feel. Love it, see it, and believe it is here. Let go of what "they" are doing. You have no control over it anyway. It serves us to stop allowing another person, or a bad situation, to live rent free in our heads. This is an important shift when practicing the law of attraction. We are responsible for our own thoughts and not the caretaker of another's negativity. What makes us happy is the business we need to mind.

One of my clients learned a very valuable lesson about her emotions during a time of sadness and loss. When the love of her life and husband of many years died prematurely, the loss was devastating. After a year or so, she finally decided she was ready for a new relationship. She knew what it was like to love deeply, to be in a committed relationship, and she wanted to have it again in her life. The new man she had been dating seemed to fit her perfect description. Although outwardly she felt blessed and fortunate to find love again, inwardly she had not resolved the pain of losing her husband. She had moved on with her life but not with her heart. I explained to her that we are more than just physical beings, that we are electromagnetic in nature. I performed a muscle test demonstrating to her that when she thought a positive thought, her arm strength would remain relatively strong against my resistance. Then I asked her to think for a moment about the husband she lost. Immediately she could not hold up her arm. I went on to explain that our minds and our bodies are very much connected, and what we think instantly affects the whole of who we are, whether we realize it or not.

Then I posed the question, "If like attracts like, and assuming that your life is a mirror reflecting what you think and feel, what kind of relationship do you think you would attract?"

She replied, "I would attract a relationship that would probably feel empty, unfulfilling, and full of hurt."

"And now describe to me how you feel in the relationship you are in."

"Although he seems like he should be the ideal man for me, I feel unfulfilled, sad, empty, and hurt much of the time."

Here was the dichotomy: she wanted to love again but she was still very much attached to the thoughts and feeling of loss. So she continued to attract more of the same empty feeling. I explained that if she truly wanted to attract love again, she needed to be willing to reframe and change that lingering part of her energy field. She seemed hesitant. She did not want to disrespect the memory of her late husband and she did not choose to feel the loss, but it is always there. I understood and rephrased what I was saying. I explained that his painful death from cancer had created a very strong reaction that had overwhelmed her. As time passed, it had become a sustaining feeling with less intensity, but it was still a part of her energy field that had remained on automatic pilot. This feeling lodged in her energy field then had the ability to duplicate itself, even if she was in a relationship with a loving partner.

"Then what do I do?" she asked helplessly.

"Can you focus on remembering the best times of your life with him as a prerequisite to attracting more of the same?"

"But when I think of him I feel the loss," she replied.

"Of course you do, but can you gently practice letting it go and allow love, rather than loss, replace it. When you do release pain from your body, that space needs to be refilled with something positive."

Her pain was an unfilled space occupying energy that kept filling up with more of the same, because much like how we have cellular memory in our tissues, we also have emotional memory in our feeling center. I suggested she replace this sorrowful space with feelings of things that made her happy and even made her laugh. She decided to commit to the process over the next two weeks, letting go of the pain and replacing it with joy. When she came back, she looked as if she had been on a fabulous vacation. Her mood, facial expression, and entire demeanor were totally uplifted. She couldn't wait to begin the next step. I started with a reminder that thoughts of loss would still arise, but she needed to honor those feelings with love and then immediately refocus on something positive. Once her emotional slate felt cleared, I asked her again to think of her husband and muscle tested her. This time she was stronger and in less than four weeks, she attracted another soulful love in her life.

There are multiple topics Jeri and I cover when addressing relationships issues. In our group seminars, our clients are encouraged to follow up with a few individual coaching sessions to determine a plan of action and identify what thought forms impede their progress. Oftentimes they find that what they initially thought of as a reasonable approach to attracting what they want is not at all what they need to address.

Jeri had a female client who felt she was in a promising relationship with a man, but she noticed he lacked a giving spirit. She decided to try the law of attraction to bring in what she wanted and became discouraged with the outcome. The couple had planned a wonderful trip to the Caribbean. Two days into the trip she found a pair of earrings she loved and he seemed to like them as well. She visualized him going back to the store and buying them for her. On the last day, he said he was going to buy a hat he had seen earlier and he would meet her back at the hotel. She was certain he was out getting her the earrings. He came back with his hat and no earrings.

She said to Jeri, "Of course I forgave him. I am a giving person and I do not know how to be any other way."

Jeri said to her, "And how well do you receive?"

She replied, "I don't get a chance to with him. I am always the one giving"

Jeri said, "Precisely, and what did you get back but another opportunity to give. You forgave him for something he did not even know he was supposed to do. Remember it starts with you.

In order to receive, you need to visualize receiving and empower how you would feel."

She agreed that her focus was on visualizing him giving her the earrings, rather than on how she would feel receiving them. With a little more introspection she realized that her relationship with giving was based on the belief that it is better to give than receive. She was attracting every opportunity to give and patting herself on the back for her generosity. This was not only a useful insight for her, but it also served as an example of the need to understand the secondary gain that keeps us attached to a way of being whenever we decide to change a pattern.

Jeri asked her to make a list of all the ways that receiving would make her feel loved. She began visualizing how she felt when she received, as well as taking the steps to acknowledge receiving from her boyfriend. Even though they were little things, she started making statements to her boyfriend like, "I love it when you make the dinner reservations," "I love it when you play with my hair," and "I love it when you comment on how I look." In return, he loved the appreciation he felt from her. Within a few months, her relationship with giving and receiving had come into balance. She graciously received his love, as well as the long awaited request to be his wife. When we choose to see the light and beauty in another, it is as if we light a candle in our own heart.

In any personal experience with financial problems, as well as in any economic downturn, everything points to lack and even if we do not experience it individually, it is difficult to avoid the collective feeling. I had a colleague tell me how she grew up in a family with little money. However, she always felt like she had everything. Both her parents had good jobs, so she believed they were well off. As she grew up, she already developed the expectation of wealth because of the private schools she attended and the lifestyle she lived. She married a professional man who earned a great deal of money and they both lived a comfortable life. She felt lucky enough to be able to buy anything she wanted and continued with that mind-set for years.

Because she never felt any of the struggles that the lack of money can bring, she continued to attract the nice things she enjoyed in life. When things turned financially downward in real estate, she was faced with money issues for the first time. She was sick over the possibility of losing everything. She explained how worrying about money had become her predominant frame of mind, and she could see how it affected her view of life adversely. One day she decided she'd had enough and was no longer going to buy into the mind-set of a collective recession. Instead, she decided to harbor the thought that there is always enough to go around. She recalled how she innocently thought she had been rich growing up and went back to that original thinking. While she and her husband still went through some rough times, they never lost anything they owned after she removed the fear and collective attitude.

I learned that same lesson and refused to buy into my own economic doom and gloom. In fact, I did just the opposite and used the law of attraction during downward times to increase my clientele. I would take a blank sheet from my planner and randomly copy down ten to twenty names and numbers from the phonebook. Then I would pencil them into my blank time slots and visualize them coming. This way I knew I always kept a full book. When a potential client would call, I would replace the name and number from the phonebook with my new appointment. Energetically, I was holding a space for them. With all the numbers I had on hold, it created the feeling that I had a waiting list. It worked! I am always busier when I energize the thought I am able to easily attract clients in stressful economic times. I believe that people who still have money will always find me.

A man told me that his company had mismanaged his retirement fund and it had lost fifty percent of its value. He was convinced he had not contributed in any possible way to this misfortune. I let him continue talking as he gave a long list of instances where unfortunate circumstances had nothing to do with him. To him, it appeared he was simply at the wrong place at the wrong time. I asked him how he had reacted. He felt he had wasted no time reacting and emphatically told me he was angry and resentful. He reiterated, with conviction, "I had no choice about any of this. I was three years old when my father lost his entire savings and killed himself. How did I attract that?" This man had faced terrible adversity and he was right, the individual circumstances were never directly his fault, but he had carried the expectation of loss and the reactivity of his anger in the backpack of his experience since he was a very young child. He never cheated a single person but himself. He never believed that good things happened to him . . . and they never did.

I remain grateful I was never robbed of my hope or steered from my belief that I could rise above adversity. This man never knew or understood what might have set him free, yet I learned and understood from him. Ironically, he was the one who asked me to tell this story in my book. He died before it was published.

We live in a universe that is governed by the quantum nature of energy, and the law of attraction will outlive us all. It remains a constant with or without our personal opinion, whether or not we believe it works. How would you live differently if you knew and believed in the law of attraction?

SONG WITHOUT END

I walked slowly across a room full of people and stood to the right of the podium. I paused for a moment and made visual contact with the audience. I held up my wrist and looked at my watch.

"Ladies and gentleman, for the next thirty seconds, I would ask that you remain absolutely silent, beginning now."

For thirty seconds I watched the discomfort in the room. Most relinquished eye contact and looked down at the floor. At the end of the time allotment, I broke the silence.

"There are 86,400 seconds in a day and for a profoundly deaf person such as myself, that is a lot of quiet time." Then I pressed play on the CD player, which played a voice barely audible and incomprehensible.

"This is how it sounded with my old hearing aids. This is how I heard each of you."

I then used only my lips to mouth several sentences.

"Can any of you tell me what I said?"

Not a single person raised their hand.

"This is how I learned to hear you, by lip-reading. Every one of us in this room, regardless of whether we hear or not, has a different experience of sound. Today, I will tell you that my experience of hearing music has once again been changed since I became a cochlear implant recipient. I thank Wendy, a deaf musician who invited me to be here today.

"How many in the audience are hearing-impaired?"

Only a few raised their hands. Most were educators or sold products to the deaf community. I continued.

For the next fifteen minutes I spoke at this national conference for the hearing-impaired about the role of music in my life. I told them about my childhood connection to the music I heard within me. I described how I first heard sounds in my mind that seemed almost celestial. I told them the story of the birthday party I attended and hoped that one day my ears could sing. I told the story about hearing the leaves blowing in the wind for the first time and wondered if they were music. I explained that I felt a musical sense watching trees bending and swaying in rhythmic patterns. I pointed out that we traditionally think of music in terms of hearing, rather than using other senses to interpret it, but that some deaf people experience the feeling of vibrations in their body. Music isn't always heard.

"Today I am honored to stand in the company of those who share my enthusiasm for music. I was asked by Wendy to talk about my own experience. I never dreamed that I would be telling an audience of predominately hearing people that I have always wanted to sing. I was the epitome of being tone deaf. There are different criteria that frame music; one of the most well known is the use of music therapy. A client of mine raised a severely disabled son who could not function on his own, yet when he heard rock music he would smile and writhe to the upbeat sounds. She could quiet his involuntary body spasms with a simple lullaby. I attended a production called *Stomp*. It did not have one traditional musical instrument in the entire production. They used trashcans, brooms, rocks, and all sorts of street paraphernalia to make music. It was a riveting performance that pulled an entire audience to their feet as they stomped and clapped their hands. We all see, hear, feel, and touch the language of music differently." As I finished my part of the presentation, I received a standing ovation. It was music to my ears, a beautiful orchestration of sound and accomplishment.

I had spent so much time struggling to be accepted as a hearing-impaired person. I had to step into another way of understanding and navigating through my life. I had to come to terms with the truth: I had been my greatest advocate with my staunch determination, but equally a detractor when I failed to accept myself unconditionally. Without self-acceptance, how could I expect to be accepted by others? I no longer needed to be like anyone else. I had an identity of my own, just like everyone else.

I enjoyed drawing from the energy of positive emotion. I was no longer consumed with playing the catch-up game. I either got it or I didn't. Before my implants, I often did not hear well enough to understand how I embarrassed myself, but I was sensitive enough to know when others were embarrassed for me. I had the option to move on and get over it or flounder in the pain and remain unhappy. There was always a choice.

I came to a much clearer understanding of how God and self-creation worked together. Just like the vibration of music, I had to feel what I was putting out and in what type of vibration I chose to remain. We are the maestros of our own making. I thought back on the evening Jeri made the funny remark on my fortieth birthday that maybe if I heard music from the inside, I could be a conductor. It led to an interesting conversation and understanding of how much music is also perception. That night she had reacted to the hip-hop band in the next room, feeling it was loud and distracting. I had felt it rumble in my body and almost rattle my teeth, but we had both thought of it as music. We all have different experiences of sound, with senses that are finely tuned and imprint our brains differently. Beethoven, who lost his hearing in adulthood, was still able to pull from his auditory memory bank and compose great music. As he once said, *"Music should strike fire from the heart of man. . . ."* I knew this was true.

My passion was the vital ingredient that rocked me out of bed each morning. I loved that my life had purpose and I could plug it into every aspect of my life. I attracted my desired reality, while intensifying my creative abilities. Much like windsurfing, we may be able to stand on the board for a time, but when we discover how to masterfully work with the wind, we soar.

Most of my friends were already married and some on the second go-round. For lack of a better term, I grew weary of the singles scene and although I never identified when, where, or even how, it dimmed in importance. I always enjoyed relationships, but when and if they ended, I did not mourn them like I had in the earlier years. I was finally okay being alone, not having a Saturday night date or a party to attend. I understood how spiritual relationships mirrored back who we really are. I welcomed that reflection as well as attracting a soul-based partnership. This was my choice for giving and receiving love. When we are in a place of allowance, we are able to receive what we intend. When we graciously accept life's creations without resistance or judgments, we allow transformation to occur. This was clearly my intent.

I respected the importance of checking in with how I felt and letting go of attachments or trying to control outcome. If the journey of a thousand miles begins with one step, I no longer felt the need to take five steps. It felt comfortable to go back to that God space of my childhood and really know it had not been the conjuring of my imagination. I still sit on my deck overlooking the lake and immerse myself in the evening's last hurrah of light before the sun sets in splendor. I never grow tired of the sounds of nature, once absent in my world of sound. I love the mellifluous chatter of birds and the graceful landing of geese on the lake, as if their arrival pays tribute to the disappearing sun. Impending storms awe me. Now I am able to hear the impetuous wind push its way through the pre-storm hush. And I hear the cracking of tree branches as they bow down or splinter off from their source. This is where the noise of nature fades with its purity into the background and that unsullied, resonating God sound pulsates in the forefront of my awareness.

Do we ever arrive at the place of being there, or is life a mere continuation and perpetuation of the dreams we envision? What was it about, beating the odds and defying the impossible that dangled the luring bait of "more"? *Now what?* I asked myself while sipping a glass of wine. I had always been a relentless questioner. *What next?* I knew the answer as soon as I asked the question. This one I had to do alone. I did not say a single word to Jeri about what was next on my agenda. I worked for months barely containing my excitement as I prepared.

When the time finally came, I anxiously waited for Jeri to arrive at my condo. I had told her nothing about why we were getting together. She rang my doorbell and although it felt like my heart was beating outside of my body, I was grinning from ear to ear.

The first thing she said was, "I know you are up to something. I can always tell."

"Could be," I replied.

I escorted her into my office and motioned for her to take a seat across from my desk. I casually meandered over to my computer and switched on my music. She had not noticed the cordless microphone and headset tucked behind my bookends. I put them on and turned to her.

"Today I make good on my promise to sing."

For the first time in my memory, Jeri was speechless.

I had searched endless hours to find the right song. I selected "This is the Moment" from the Broadway musical *Jekyll and Hyde*. These amazing lyrics spoke to me as if they had been written solely for this occasion. My voice teacher Laurie had coached me for months and I was finally ready.

I filled my lungs with a deep and cleansing breath and then exhaled any trace of longing from my past. I inched the microphone closer to my lips in foreplay. The overture ended and on perfect cue and pitch . . . I reached deep inside and gave birth to my very first song. I will not share with you the lyrics of the song, but its message, in my own words, as I connected to my heart.

At last this was my day.
My struggle was over.

My inner critic silenced.
My yesterday, the past.
My tomorrow not here.
My moment was NOW.

As I continued to sing, I gained momentum.

I knew this time I would prevail.
Nothing was ever impossible.
I believed.
I saw.
I knew.
It became.
I claimed it.
I felt in total synchronicity with the present,
It had all come together in "this moment."
Daydreams made real.
Completion fueled by desire,
Connection to all there is,
Oneness with God.
And the rebirth of joy.
TODAY, I HAD DEFIED ALL THE ODDS!
This was indeed my unsurpassed moment.
A miracle conceived in my childhood dreams.
My voice uplifted in song.

I don't remember actually hearing the notes as I sang. This was my crescendo, the very moment I raised my hand to impossibility and sent it on its way. The music ended. The song was over. My promise fulfilled.

Yes! . . . These Ears Could Sing!

I looked over at Jeri and could see that tears were streaming down her face.

"Mike, oh my god that was so unbelievable . . . so beautiful. You did it! I thought you had given up."

She could not stop repeating those words. Choking back my own emotions, I thanked her for all her help, her wisdom, and most of all, for believing in me. I had seen this moment so many times. Jeri then smiled and with her usual joking repartee said, "You do know don't you, that *Jekyll and Hyde* is about the ramblings of a madman?"

"Well then, I would say that suits me just fine," I replied.

"You have come a long way from Cinderella," she laughed.

"And it sure beats waving a magic wand," I assured her.

This would always remain my long awaited and triumphant . . . song without end!

NEW BEGINNINGS

epilogue

You will be amused to know, I still mishear words. When it was suggested to me to write an epilogue, instead I heard "epitaph" and thought of the old spiritual hymn lyrics, "How Can I Keep from Singing?" The first time I sang like everyone else in church, I mistakenly bellowed out the refrain, "How could I keep from sinking?" Today, the more subtle nuances of communication in my life are still very much a work in progress. As I look back to my first thought when I wondered if these ears could sing, I embarked on a journey of imagination seeded with the knowing that one day I would. This epilogue is the next leg in my journey of new beginnings.

I am happy to report I received a second cochlear implant in my other ear and soon thereafter an upgraded reimplantation of my first device. This extraordinary technology has taken another colossal leap, with an even greater capacity to assimilate the magnificent gift of sound to both of my ears. From the uncertain little boy that carried a primitive voice box around his neck, I am both humbled and grateful to be "a bilaterally bionic man." I will hear . . . and I do.

Jeri and I are now partners in our own coaching business, Coming Attractions. We work individually with clients in crafting their very best life by applying the universal law of attraction. The power of imagination has no limits when you deliberately cause life to happen. We teach seminars in attracting a life free of the notion that the circumstances or conditions are ever without purpose or beyond your control. How you react to them defines what you experience. You must think it, be it, see it, and feel it, to ever own it. Compel yourself to become the magnet that attracts your dreams.

COMING ATTRACTIONS, INC.

presents

Mike Gannon & Jeri Costa

Please visit our website at:
http://www.OfficialLawOfAttraction.com

Email: Mike@OfficialLawOfAttraction.com
Jeri@OfficialLawOfAttraction.com

Contact us at: 888-923-3339

OUR SERVICES:

- Personal coaching by Mike or Jeri
- Group law of attraction coaching
- Tele-seminars
- Motivational speaking

You are an inexplicable act of quantum creation.

With the spark of a single thought,

conceived with clarity and felt with conviction,

you can create your desired reality.

"Imagination Is Everything"
It is the preview of life's coming attractions
– Albert Einstein

9 780982 923504